The New Work of Dogs

The New Work of Dogs

Tending to Life, Love,

and Family

Jon Katz

LARGE PRINT

This large print edition published in 2003 by
RB Large Print
A division of Recorded Books
A Haights Cross Communications Company
270 Skipjack Road
Prince Frederick, MD 20678

First published by Villard Books, 2003

Publisher's Cataloging In Publication Data
(Prepared by Donohue Group, Inc.)

Katz, Jon.
  The new work of dogs: tending to life, love, and family / Jon Katz.

    p. ; cm.

  ISBN: 1-4025-6387-6

1. Katz, Jon. 2. Dogs—New Jersey—Montclair—Anecdotes. 3. Dogs—Behavior—New
Jersey—Montclair—Anecdotes. 4. Human-animal relationships—New Jersey—Montclair—
Anecdotes. 5. Large type books. I. Title.

SF426.2 .K386 2003b
636.7/009749/31

Typeset by Palimpsest Book Production Limited
Polmont, Stirlingshire, Scotland
Printed in the United States of America
by Bang Printing
3323 Oak Street
Brainerd, Minnesota 56401

**This Large Print Book carries the
Seal of Approval of N.A.V.H.**

For Carolyn Wilki,

a great friend and a ferocious advocate

for a better relationship

between humans and dogs

It begins with my dog, now dead, who all his long life carried about in his head the brown eyes of my father, keen, loving, accepting, sorrowful, whatever; they were Daddy's all right, handed on, except for their phosphorescent gleam tunneling the night which I have to concede was a separate gift.

—from *"The Retrieval System"*
by MAXINE KUMIN

The New Work of Dogs

PREFACE

Mills reservation is a heavily wooded county park that stretches along the hilly ridge marking the northwest boundary of my town, Montclair, New Jersey. A series of trails meanders through the forest, some offering spectacular views of Manhattan, just a half-hour's drive east. The park, designed by the famed Frederick Law Olmsted, winds across 157 acres.

Like almost every bit of surviving greenery in northern New Jersey, this space feels under continuous siege from developers. Another hideous, overpriced house seems to pop up on its perimeter every month. The trails grow more crowded with families herding kids, with retirees out for walks, all thirsting for some green, a quiet place to stroll and gaze out at the majestic skyline across the Hudson.

Mills is also unofficial headquarters for the town's thriving dog universe. The first wave starts arriving at dawn: solitary people who want to walk alone with their canine pals; people with enormous or unreliable dogs who need a run before the park fills up; commuters who need to get their walks in before they hit the 7:10; dog-walking and doggie play groups led by people whose fanny packs are filled with balls, treats, bottled water (for the dogs), and poop bags.

The rescue people stick to the narrower, less-traveled paths, keeping careful watch over dogs freshly liberated from shelters or found on streets; saved from death, abuse, neglect, or abandonment; in various stages of physical and emotional rehab. They talk constantly to the sometimes nervous dogs, assessing the latest arrivals, watching for signs of illness or other trouble, soothing them, teaching them their new names, routines, commands.

The biggest invasion happens after work. Until dark, the woods echo with barks. People passing on the paths often introduce their dogs, though not usually themselves. It's a friendly group nonetheless, trading information about newly discovered spots—lakes, trails, patches of woods—where they can take dogs to run. Dogs who spend time here tend to grow fond of people, whose pockets are generally stuffed with biscuits to share.

Mills provides a neat microcosm of America's canine experience: more dogs than ever, fewer places where they can go, fewer ways they can interact with the world.

Everyone except the newest newcomers is a scarred veteran of the struggle between dog lovers, the "civilian" population, and the county authorities, who launch sporadic ineffective crusades to drive the dogs and their people back, or at least contain them. In this corner of the megalopolis, as in most places, much of what dogs naturally do—run loose, gather in packs, chase after one another, have sex, roll in smelly stuff—is frowned upon or illegal.

The best estimates I've seen—from the Humane Society of the United States—indicate that non-dog households outnumber dog households at about a sixty-forty ratio, which is probably why dog people lose most of their intensifying civic struggles over leash laws and dog bans, curbs and prohibitions.

Dog owners are a stubborn lot, however, and Mills is one of the last treasured redoubts in this populated region for people who want to give their dogs a real run or a chance to play with other dogs. It draws Labs, terriers, rescued greyhounds and whippets, poodles and pit bulls, rottweilers and "Heinz 57" mongrels. The purebreds and show dogs trot and run alongside the mutts; the high-strung working breeds sniff and woof at the family pets.

There, on any given day, you might meet Ginnie, a deaf pit bull who was shot in the head. Her owner, a lawyer named John who normally hates dogs, accidentally struck her with his car as she wandered, wounded, along a street in Belleville, just outside Newark. He took her in, to his own astonishment and the horror of his wife and neighbors, and now adores her. He hates dogs more than ever, he insists; it's just that he loves Ginnie.

To see grumpy John communicating with Ginnie by stomping his foot—she can feel the vibrations—and then gesturing elaborately while she looks at him lovingly, wags her tail, and learns to sit and stay—responding more quickly than most hearing pets—is to glimpse the amazing emotional landscape that exists between some people and their dogs.

You might, alternatively, run into Sadie, the one-eyed shepherd-husky mix who was thrown from an overpass onto Interstate 280. She bounced off a speeding car and landed on the shoulder alongside a BMW driven by an ABC News producer, who proceeded to spend $4,000 on the veterinary surgery that saved her and gave her a phosphorescent eye-patch that glows in the dark—useful for locating her at night but occasionally unnerving to passersby. Sadie and Ginnie have become friends, and the sight of the two of them jogging along a path at dusk is memorable.

You might also encounter Shadow, the English sheepdog imported from Europe, strolling imperiously along on a leash festooned with ribbons won in herding trials and competitions. Or Ditz, the aptly named tiny Chihuahua who scoots safely between the legs of Moose, a mighty but genial bull mastiff. Moose is not to be confused with another mastiff who walks in Mills, accompanied by a bright-red parrot who rides on his collar, squawking curses at other dogs.

But it was Rushmore and his owner, Kate DeLand, who first planted the germ of the idea that became this book. Arriving at Mills with my border collies one fall morning, I came across these two standing at the edge of the parking area, both looking bewildered and uneasy.

Rushmore, a blue-eyed, classically beautiful German shepherd, paid my circling dogs no attention at all. He seemed, in fact, to be looking right past us.

"Excuse me," Kate ventured. She was braver. "This is our first time here. I'm not sure what to do. Is there any protocol?" She did look out of place: she was wearing too-tailored wool pants and an expensive-looking sweater, and she was equipped with none of the dog paraphernalia most people toted through the Reservation.

She was right to ask; a complex set of rules and conventions govern Mills, a critical understanding anywhere dog people congregate in crowded urban or suburban areas. In their own self-interest, responsible dog owners are a tough, self-policing lot.

First, I told her, the wealthy residents of the adjacent new housing developments didn't like running into so many dogs and were calling the county sheriff to complain.

The police, therefore, had launched another

of their periodic assaults, hiding in the woods in SUVs, popping out now and then to issue dire warnings or write hundred-and-fifty-dollar tickets when they spotted dogs being walked off-leash. Signs prohibiting dogs had sprouted all over the park.

The dog people seemed the more determined of the combatants; they'd never quit. Non-dog lovers had other parks to stroll through, but for the dog people, it had come down to Mills. They knew the hard-pressed county cops wouldn't invest manpower in dog patrols for long. And they were used to guerrilla warfare.

They had taken to blowing whistles and shouting warnings when they spotted the police. Two groups even carried walkie-talkies and stationed spotters at the park entrance to spread the word when sheriff's deputies arrived, so that everybody could leash up.

In general, the regulars were cautious, I told Kate, letting dogs off-leash only if they were reliable with people, if they'd been socialized to behave well with other dogs, if they were well-trained and under control. They cleaned up after their dogs, avoided walking in large packs in the more heavily trafficked areas of the Reservation. If they encountered elderly or disabled people, or young children, or anybody who looked remotely uneasy, they leashed their dogs or moved them off the paths. Anyone whose dog bit another dog—as opposed to the brief, harmless dust-ups that are a relatively normal part of canine communications—was expected to leash it permanently.

Dog people had little patience with people who gasped, "He's never done that before," or who disdained training as a waste of time or money, even as their dogs became increasingly neurotic, loud, or aggressive. Things were tough enough for well-behaved dogs. People who didn't want to bother to control their dogs should go elsewhere.

I warned Kate, though, that some people—plenty, in fact—weren't especially responsible. They didn't clean up after dogs, forcing people to step in or around smelly poop; they brought dogs of uncertain disposition, frightening parents and kids and mountain bikers and hikers. I'd run into a man who'd brought four rescue dogs fresh from a New York shelter and let them loose along a trail; several had attacked and mauled a passing beagle.

But Kate still looked anxious and unhappy, uncertain even about how to attach Rushmore's leash to his collar. She'd been tossing the shepherd an oversized soccer ball, and he kept giving her a woebegone look. She might try a smaller, bouncier ball, I suggested, one he could pick up and retrieve.

Rushmore wasn't exactly her dog, she eventually explained; she wasn't really a dog person. He had been the birthday present she bought her husband not long before he collapsed of a heart attack six months ago; he died soon after, at forty-four. She'd considered sending the dog back to the breeder, but couldn't do it. She chose to keep him, she said, because it was what her husband would have wanted, because her husband had loved the dog so much. But she seemed grim, duty-bound.

Rushmore had the heroic gaze and dignity of the breed. But clearly, something was wrong. Kate seemed merely to tolerate him. Perhaps even the sight of him was painful.

I invited her to join us on our walk so she could learn the rituals of Mills; with relief, she agreed.

Rushmore showed little interest in any of the things most dogs love to do—eat awful things, roll in muck, sniff other dogs, greet humans, bound majestically through the trees. He even refused the treats people offered.

When we rounded a turn along the trail and three barky mutts dashed up for a sniff, Rushmore impassively allowed their inquiries, then moved on.

But she was determined to see this through, Kate was saying, to learn what she had to learn and to do right by Rushmore, thus honoring her husband's memory and keeping part of him alive. "No matter what," she said.

Well, commitment is half the battle. And there was a lot of feeling there: she seemed near tears as she talked about the dog. She didn't quite know what to do with him, or how to fill the void her husband had left in the dog's life, but she wanted to try, even as she was recovering from her own grief and working to glue her life back together.

We decided to meet at Mills Wednesday mornings so Kate could walk with me and my dogs, plus whoever else we picked up along the way, and learn the ropes. And the next couple of months brought a poignant transformation. Although I'd expected her to disappear after a week or two, she showed up religiously. She and Rushmore took long walks, mornings and evenings. She hired a trainer, an important step. Many people in Montclair with expensive, eighty-pound working dogs don't think it worth the additional three or four hundred dollars to train them—or even bother to read a book and do the job themselves—and tolerate the unhappy results, from aggression and incessant barking to chewed-up wardrobes.

But Kate took Rushmore to a highly regarded dog-training center named St. Hubert's, in Madison, to do agility and obedience work. She taught him to fetch, which made it easier to exercise him; he took to carrying a small blue or red ball through the park.

She practiced what they learned, using food and toys and praise—Rushmore was also developing a keen interest in beef jerky—to reward him when he came, sat, stayed, or made eye contact. He didn't show much initial interest in romping—like many German shepherds, Rushmore had true gravitas—but soon he and several retrievers had staked out a mudhole. More important, he was showing interest in Kate, swiveling his head sharply when she called his name, walking back to check on how she was doing.

By winter, she reported that Rushmore "meant the world" to her, that she could never have gotten through Stan's death without him, that he had pulled her out of herself, kept her exercising, eased her loneliness, given her a powerful reason to keep going.

"At first, Rushmore reminded me of my husband's death, and I could hardly stand to look at him," she confessed. "Then he reminded me of my husband, which was different. He somehow became a way for me to heal." In fact, she was startled when the grief therapist she'd been seeing suggested that she bring Rushmore to their sessions, but she did. "I would talk and cry with him sitting at my feet, and he just became part of my recovery. And then, the frosting on the cake, we started having fun together. My girlfriends were wonderful—they worked hard to be there for me—but they couldn't curl up with me on cold winter nights while I sat on the sofa in my sweats. They couldn't share an empty house."

It wasn't the first time that I'd seen a relationship evolve that amounted to more than a human's acquiring a pet.

Watching these two made me want to write about the extraordinary connection between Americans and their dogs.

Over the past couple of years, I've spoken with

hundreds of dog owners—plus breeders, rescuers, trainers, behaviorists, and psychiatrists. Our discussions have ranged from half-hour sidewalk encounters to extensive interviews in people's homes and backyards. It's been an education.

I've chosen to focus here on a handful of people and their dogs—who all live in Montclair, or close by—because they best embody the theory I've been developing and researching: that the new work of dogs is attending to the emotional lives of Americans, many of whom feel increasingly disconnected from one another.

That isn't the whole story, of course. Some people get dogs for simpler reasons—for company, security, hunting, or work—with few psychological motives. But more people than ever see dogs as partners or surrogates as they deal with serious problems in their past or current lives.

As I explored this idea as a journalist and author, many of the people I met let me into their homes and lives for as long as it took to capture their stories. That sometimes required just a few visits; in other cases, our involvement stretched on for months as I followed their dog relationships from puppyhood through training, maturity, and beyond.

I went with people to pick up puppies at breeders and accompanied these duos on walks and to vets' offices. I went with rescue teams to shelters and adoption fairs, then followed the dogs as they made their way into their new homes and lives, sometimes successfully, sometimes not.

In researching this book, I've also drawn heavily on the writings of sociologists, dog trainers and behaviorists, and psychologists, psychiatrists, and psychoanalysts, especially those who've studied attachment theory as it relates to people and their pets.

The attachment view of relationships, first articulated by the British psychiatrist John Bowlby and increasingly embraced by mental health professionals, concerns the seminal importance of the way human beings attach to their primary caretakers (or don't) in the earliest stages of life.

This process has a profound impact on human beings; it can help explain human relationships and emotions across the life span. It also helps explain people's powerful attachments to their dogs.

The first person to call my attention to the connection between attachment theory and dogs' roles was psychiatrist Debra Katz of the University of Kentucky at Lexington. She'd read my previous book, *A Dog Year*, about my relationship with a troubled border collie, and e-mailed me. "Maybe I'm off my rocker," she wrote, "but the work you did with Devon is the kind of work we do in attachment-based psychotherapy involving parents and children. I gave your book to one of our senior child psychiatrists here who agreed that your dog had 'an attachment disorder' when you got him and that you did a true psychotherapy of sorts with him."

As we corresponded, and as she and her fellow researchers sent me stacks of books and studies, bells went off. This was what I'd been seeing day after day—people deeply enmeshed with their dogs, often acting out emotional issues, aware of the depth of feeling they had for their animals but rarely of the emotional history or context. Psychiatrists I contacted at several other universities and in several cities agreed that Dr. Katz's observation was astute and significant.

Attachment seems a critical element in the new work of dogs, a means of replaying old scenarios and, sometimes, closing old wounds. Suddenly I had an intellectual context for some of the powerful stories I was watching unfold. Attachment theory, I came to believe, is a significant part of the unfolding story of dogs in America. So is social disconnection.

The emotional landscape between people and their dogs has proved rich and riveting. The intensifying emotional connection, the trend toward viewing dogs as members of our families and other kinds of human surrogates, is striking. Most dog owners know it and freely admit it. So do vets, trainers, breeders, and, especially, the pet industry, which markets dog products the same way marketers push clothes and toys for children. Studies show that a growing number of people feel, correctly or not, that they get more support from their dogs than from their spouses or parents.

This same emotional punch led to unexpected difficulties, however. As people began to consider and explore their feelings for their dogs, they soon ended up talking frankly about *people*: parents, siblings, kids, spouses. A few simply felt silly acknowledging how much they loved and depended on their dogs, an easy target for ridicule and, at times, a painful subject. Members of rescue groups worried about local statutes restricting the number of dogs per household and forbidding off-leash walking and other activities they sometimes engaged in.

So at their request, I've changed the names of many of the people in this book; in a couple of instances, I've rendered them unidentifiable by changing other details as well. All the people I depict are real, however, as are their dogs and experiences; no anecdote is invented or substantially altered.

Sometimes such stories end happily for the dogs and the people; sometimes not. As I've spent time talking with and reading about people and their dogs, it's been striking to see how little we've learned about this landmark evolution from the animal's perspective. Dogs seem a blank canvas on which we can paint anything we want, sometimes to their disadvantage.

Moving and powerful examples abound of dogs working hard and profoundly helping the humans they live with. Like almost everybody else, however, I've also seen dogs placed in impossible, even disturbing, situations, overwhelmed by the pressure put on them to fill complex emotional roles in their owners' lives. In part, this book is an effort to remember that dogs are voiceless, that a critical part of having dogs is emotional responsibility: learning how to understand them and, when necessary, to speak and act on their behalf.

Once again, Rushmore brought this drama vividly to mind. After several months, he and Kate disappeared from Mills. Their relationship, I concluded, must have evolved to the point that they didn't need company or training tips any longer.

That was partly correct. Nearly a year after we'd first met, my dogs and I were startled to see Rushmore bounding up the trail behind us. In contrast to our first encounter, he appeared happy to see me and my treat-stuffed pockets, and especially happy to see my dogs, licking them both and wagging in greeting.

Behind him came Kate and a lanky man she introduced as her fiancé, Hank. She hadn't been to Mills in months, she explained, since this "new relationship" had entered her life.

As we talked, Rushmore drifted down the trail and sniffed at some bushes, ignoring all of us. Apparently he was no longer "the world" to Kate, no longer the thing that kept her going, a bulwark against pain and loneliness.

Hank, a perfectly nice guy, made it clear that he wasn't a dog person. He ignored my border collies—dog people almost never do—and cracked jokes about Rushmore's bad breath, shedding, and slobbering, all traits dog people take as givens and rarely even notice. Kate, along with Rushmore, had moved in with him, and this didn't bode well for the dog's future. Hank suggested that the dog was messing up his otherwise tidy and attractive home. If Kate stayed with Hank, I feared, Rushmore would be gone.

When I knelt down and called him, Rushmore came waggling over; I scratched his ears while he licked my face, his big tail swinging. He had gained a lot of weight since we'd last met; Kate explained that she just didn't have time to exercise him as much.

Truthfully, I didn't know what to feel. I was happy for Kate, a kind and lovely person recovering from a shocking loss. She had done what humans in her situation ought to try to do—she'd found a human to attach to. But what about Rushmore? Would he become unnoticed and unwanted in this new emotional configuration? Perhaps even be given away, sent to a shelter or rescue group?

"Rushmore, let's go," Hank yelled impatiently,

after we'd finished our conversation. Rushmore seemed not to have heard him. He went galloping off into the woods with a passing golden retriever and didn't look back.

CHAPTER 1

DOGVILLE, U.S.A.

As gracious as the shady township of Montclair is, as hip and pricey as it is becoming, there's no escaping the fact that it sits squarely in New Jersey, a beacon in the vast sea of ugly industrial and suburban sprawl that is the state's most famous characteristic. Malls and condo complexes lap at its lush borders from every side.

But Montclair remains an enclave of old homes on streets lined with giant oaks and maples planted eighty years ago, some of which fall in every big storm. It has more movie screens than hardware stores and more Thai and Japanese restaurants than fast-food outlets. It is utterly obsessed with education and the present and future development of its much-attended-to children.

Founded as a summer retreat for wealthy New Yorkers, it also reflects the sobering disparities in wealth that characterize contemporary America. Along the ridges of the Watchung Hills, the living rooms of vast, meticulously maintained mansions have clear views of the Manhattan skyline. In the South End, small apartments and houses are home to most of the town's poor residents.

For reasons few can recall, Montclair is actually divided into two parts—Upper Montclair and plain old Montclair. The two Montclairs share the same government, municipal services, and school system, but Upper Montclair is richer and whiter, with an upscale shopping area and its own zip code.

Partly because of its proximity to the cultural and media institutions along Manhattan's West Side, Montclair attracts rafts of writers, artists, editors, journalists, TV producers, and other media people. So even minor civic squabbles tend to make their way onto the pages of *The New York Times*, since half the people who work at the paper live here, or so it sometimes seems.

Montclair is, for much of the surrounding area, a Manhattan surrogate, a place to go for indie movies or fusion cuisine.

It's commonplace to go out for a walk and see a commercial being shot at the picturesque train station down the street, to encounter a *New Yorker* writer or a soap-opera star at church or at the organic-foods supermarket, or to spot Yogi Berra, the New York Yankee legend, getting his SUV serviced downtown.

Less-celebrated residents commute into Manhattan or out to the exurban office complexes and business parks that stain the surrounding countryside. A growing number sit by their computers all day in home offices, visited at intervals by UPS and Fed-Ex trucks, with whose drivers they are on a first-name basis.

Newcomers—drawn by improved rail lines into the city, the town's growing rep for sophisticated cultural offerings, and its deserved tolerance for diversity (all driving real estate prices through the clouds)—are streaming in from Brooklyn and Manhattan. They bring an informed, somewhat combative, politically correct edge to the civic life of a town that was fairly intense to start with.

Montclair is also something of a social laboratory, where trends and traits pop up before hitting the rest of the country. Moms leaving home for work, kids strollered around by nannies, dads staying at home, then moms growing disillusioned with the workplace and returning home to raise their kids—we could track it all as we walked our dogs. We saw the influx of families with two mommies or two daddies. We watched the town become a magnet for interracial couples. An already successful and settled black professional class expanded. The Wall Streeters stayed with their Beamers and Mercedes.

In fact, Montclair seems to include some of everything and everyone. WASP country-clubbers live more or less harmoniously with Jews and blacks; single professionals from Manhattan coexist with kid-crazed boomers from Brooklyn; ardent liberal professors and Republicans and conservatives manage to get along; lesbian and gay families mingle with Asian immigrants.

Of Montclair's 38,977 inhabitants, 23,000 are white and 13,000 African-American. The 2000 census also found 73 American Indian or Alaskan natives, 1,300 Asians, and nearly 2,000 Hispanics.

Maybe they get along reasonably well because there is no mistaking what Montclair is primarily about: children. Kids are why most people move here or stay here, why they sound off angrily at school board meetings and gather intelligence on math teachers and soccer coaches with the same ruthlessness and determination that archaeologists comb desert sites for dinosaur bones.

Day and night, station wagons, SUVs, and vans zip back and forth between friends' houses and hockey and lacrosse games, karate classes and art lessons. For Montclair's hyperstimulated middle-class children, a day without a positive educational or social experience is—well, there hardly are such days.

But high up on the list of things this polyglot town cares most deeply about—close behind real estate values—comes dogs.

Montclair, it turns out, *is* Dogville, U.S.A. According to the American Veterinary Association's *U.S. Pet Ownership and Demographic Sourcebook*, Montclair almost perfectly exemplifies the American dog-owning population—educated, affluent, child-centered, and middle-class to the core.

Dog ownership increases as family income rises. Nearly 40 percent of American households with annual incomes of $60,000 or more own a dog, compared with fewer than a quarter of households with less than $25,000 in income.

More than three-quarters of dog owners nation-wide are home owners, and dog owners are much more likely to be highly educated than the population as a whole. This is Montclair.

As is obvious on TV every night, dogs have become part of the American Dream package, that vision of supposed success and joy that includes a house, a patch of lawn, kids, and a car or two. An affectionate canine companion completes the picture.

In Montclair, people focus on their dogs with much the same intensity they apply to their children, the difference being that dogs can't play sports, take music lessons, or apply to college, fortunately for them.

I've been walking dogs—first Clarence, a golden retriever; then two yellow Labs named Julius and Stanley; now two border collies named Devon and Homer—in and around Montclair for nearly two decades.

So have a lot of other people, raising all the policy issues that have cropped up in every town with dogs: Should dogs walk off-leash? Should they be permitted to run freely in parks, or, for that matter, be admitted to parks at all? How much barking constitutes a nuisance? Should people be permitted to own so-called "dangerous" breeds like pit bulls? How vigorously should the police enforce clean-up laws? What if people want to own more than one dog or two?

Such questions have become so sensitive that what a big-city newspaper would refer to as "a senior police official" would agree to meet with me only on condition of anonymity. He also insisted on leaving the jurisdiction: we met at the Eagle Rock Diner in adjacent West Orange. "In my shoes," he told me in a hushed voice over coffee, "there is just no percentage in talking publicly about dogs. Every dog call is bad. Either there's a nasty biter loose, or some dog ran away, or there's a dogfight, or somebody's dog is barking late at night. It's nothing but trouble. Whatever you do, you lose. People will fight harder for their dogs than they do for themselves."

The township issued 1,049 licenses for dogs in 2001, but officials think at least three times that number are in residence without licenses. Although local ordinances require vaccinations and licensure, the senior police official confided what dog owners already know: this isn't high on the cops' list of unlawful activities, so the law gets widely ignored.

The numbers fluctuate, of course. Trainers and walkers and groomers talk about "Christmas dogs," the legions of adorably beribboned puppies placed under trees that will inevitably mean an upswing in their business a few months hence.

6

Like the rest of the town, the registered dog population is diverse. But among the properly licensed dogs are, in round numbers, 50 beagles, 150 golden retrievers, 200 Labs and Lab mixes, 20 German pointers, and a dozen cairn terriers along with hundreds of mixed and indefinable breeds.

Because dog ownership correlates with class, since they are expensive to own, Montclair may have more thoroughbreds than many towns; despite its mix of incomes, it remains a pre-dominantly upper-middle-class community. But people's attitudes and feelings about their pets are the same, regardless of income.

It's stunning just how much the dog experience has changed in the past few decades. Years ago, people went to the pound to find a dog, or got a puppy from a friend's or neighbor's litter. Those who bought purebreds or boutique breeds were a privileged minority, their well-born dogs an affectation.

Dog training was little known and little needed, since most dogs merely wandered their neighborhoods and were seldom walked on leashes. Mailmen and children got bitten from time to time, but it hardly ever made the news. Fighting breeds were almost unheard-of. People surely loved their dogs, but by contemporary standards, few spent much time or money on them. Dogs were in the background, not at the center, of family life. They slept in the basement or—unthinkable today—in a backyard doghouse, chased after cars and other dogs, ate table scraps.

They came and went. Some got hit by cars, others ran off or were put down when they got sick or old. When that happened, people went to the pound for another dog. Beyond the initial round of puppy shots, people rarely invested much in veterinary care.

Often much loved and fondly remembered, dogs were not treated as family members, according to behaviorists who have studied human-animal bonds. Nor did they have playdates, a phenomenon fairly common in Montclair today. The notion that they were a part of one's deepest emotional experiences would have been a joke.

The old-timers in Montclair remember.

"We had a dog on this same block thirty years ago," Irv, the retired elementary school teacher across the street, was reminiscing one afternoon. "We let it out in the morning, it came back a couple of times during the day and then at night. We fed it leftovers from dinner. We had no idea where he went all day. We used to joke he had a girlfriend out there, maybe another family.

"My dog used to rampage through the neighbor's garbage all the time, so I'd have to go over and clean up. He went after the mailman a couple of times, but that wasn't unusual; I never heard of anybody getting sued over a dog bite. Course, we didn't have these vicious kinds of dogs running around, either, and I never heard of anybody being killed or maimed badly by a dog. And if you ever would've asked me to carry a bag around with dog poop, I'da slugged you. But there were dogs running loose all over the place. Now they call the police. . . .

"One day he just went out in the morning and never came back. Great dog."

But my observations and research have persuaded me that this relationship has changed. Montclair is a politically conscious place, and, according to local vets, pet-store owners, and shelter groups, many of its residents prefer a "rescue" dog to one bought from a breeder or pet store. In fact, it seems that every other dog here is a rescue dog, "probably abused," their owners often say. Like the idea of rescue, the popularization of the abused dog is new and growing more pronounced.

Many of the expatriate New Yorkers who move to town feel drawn to the idea of saving a helpless creature, particularly one perceived as having been mistreated. Dog trainers and behaviorists will tell you there are plenty of abused dogs, but that many perfectly healthy and normal dogs show many of the same symptoms—cowering, hiding, trembling—when simply introduced to new homes.

Rescue fantasies and motivations are familiar to therapists, especially in people who were themselves mistreated or ached for escape from loneliness and alienation. Rescues sometimes can also be an outlet for political frustrations. Social problems seem overwhelming, government remote, civics fractious and complex. But as a magazine editor in my neighborhood explained, "I can't seem to do much for people these days, so the least I can do is rescue a dog."

And there are many to rescue, according to the Humane Society of the United States. Every year, between 8 and 10 million dogs enter the U.S. shelter system. Some 4 to 5 million are killed because there are no homes for them.

In towns like Montclair, where everything makes a political statement and children are always being taught societal lessons, it means something to have rescued a dog as opposed to simply having bought or adopted one.

Something buried in the psyches of certain contemporary Americans needs to alter animals' fates, and leads them to see those they've rescued as having suffered grievously. And who is to say otherwise? Dogs can't testify.

These emotional crosscurrents may help explain why there are so many more dogs than there used to be. A clipping from *The Washington Post* in the late 1950s suggests that there were then between 12 and 15 million dogs in America. In 1991, the American Veterinary Medical Association reported about 51 million dogs in the United States. Eleven years later, a Humane Society of the United States estimate—and of course, in the absence of a dog census these are all estimates—now finds approximately 68 million owned dogs nationwide. Forty percent of U.S.

households include at least one dog, and 20 percent of those dogs were adopted from animal shelters.

I don't think it's coincidental that the explosion in the American dog population occurred at almost the same time that TV usage also began to skyrocket.

As Americans have grown transfixed by entertainment technologies, sociologists believe they've found it more difficult to make contact with other people. America's common spaces and traditions—downtown parks, coffee shops and taverns, town meetings and bowling leagues—have declined, eroded by the population's growing mobility.

It's interesting that my neighbor Irv, who saw dogs so differently, knew all the kids and people on the block and could still recite the family history of each house until about a decade ago. Now few of our neighbors can name more than a handful of the people who live on the street. They have little to do with local government, and vote sporadically, at best. In the evenings and on weekends, they go their own ways. Their kids are repeatedly warned against talking to people they don't know.

It's reached the point that in a Cleveland suburb a city councilman actually inaugurated a program by which people on a block could meet their neighbors. Two or three nights a week, residents were encouraged to sit on their porches or front stoops and introduce themselves to one another. "It isn't that we aren't friendly," one resident told a TV reporter. "We just are so busy coming and going that we don't see one another."

Political scientists have noticed the estrangement. In *Civic Engagement in American Democracy*, Theda Skocpol and Morris P. Fiorina write that millions of Americans are drawing back from involvement in politics and community affairs. Sociologist Robert D. Putnam, author of *Bowling Alone: The Collapse and Revival of American Community*, agrees, adding that entertainment technologies like television—the average American now spends more than four hours a day in front of the set—have kept people at home evenings and weekends, away from the activities that used to bring them in contact with one another.

Other recent surveys show that nearly all Americans who are online are devoting more time to their computers every year. Depending on age, they spend two to five hours online daily—exclusive of work—to e-mail, shop, and play games.

Meanwhile, Putnam, Susan J. Phar, and Russell J. Dalton argue (in *Disaffected Democracies: What's Troubling the Trilateral Countries?*) that public confidence in leaders and institutions in the United States and other democratic countries has sunk to an all-time low. They cite survey after survey—especially nearly annual polling done by the Harris Poll since 1966—showing that citizens have detached from political parties and processes, that they believe that the people running their countries don't care what happens to them, that people with power take advantage of it, that they've been "left out" of governing, that the rich get richer and the poor get poorer, and that "what you think doesn't count very much anymore."

These attitudes, say Putnam and Pharr and Dalton, grow more pronounced every year—one more reason, perhaps, why people turn elsewhere for connection, companionship, and a sense of well-being.

At about the same time television and computer screens became pervasive, the emotional and familial lives of Americans also grew more complex. The extended family began to shrink and disintegrate. Divorce rates shot up and remain high. The medical advances that helped people live longer also meant that the number of widowed and disabled rose sharply. Americans moved more frequently, leaving their communities. The number of single-person households continues to increase, along with the number of childless couples.

The nature of the workplace, too, has radically changed. Tens of millions of people have lost their jobs in the last two decades. In *The Corrosion of Character: The Personal Consequences of Work in the New Capitalism*, sociologist Richard Sennett argues that the nature of modern workplaces directly affects people's emotional lives. The Darwinian rules of the new economy have eviscerated any sense of workplace security, loyalty, or peace of mind. A frenzy of mergers, acquisitions, layoffs, and down-sizings has led to increased isolation and vulnerability. Healthcare and retirement costs have become a central personal and financial concern.

Such changes and losses cropped up again and again in the interviews and encounters I've had with dog people. They got their dogs for their kids, some say. But many acknowledge they were lonely and wanted to get out more, that they felt isolated in their marriages or after a divorce or a layoff, that they were anxious to nurture, save, or love something, that they felt disconnected and were in need of emotional support, that they just needed a living thing to take a walk with.

A half-century ago, many of these motivations wouldn't have been commonly articulated as reasons to get a dog. But during many interviews, it seemed that the people I was talking to had holes of one sort or another in their lives; they were hoping that a dog might fill it.

Accordingly, we treat our pets very differently than our grandparents did. Most pet owners, reports *American Demographic* magazine, refer to themselves as "Mommy" or "Daddy."

Americans spent $29 billion on their pets in 2001, according to a pet-industry analyst at Business Communications Company, up from $17 billion in 1994. By 2005, the figure is projected to reach $34 billion.

In fact, an American Animal Hospital Association survey found that three-quarters of pet owners would go into debt to provide for their animals' well-being. Nearly a third—and almost *half* of all single people—say that of everyone in their lives, they rely most on their pets for companionship and affection, a Yankelovich survey for *American Demographics* reveals. Four percent call pets more faithful than friends and 2 percent agree that their pets are more reliable than their parents.

Sixty-five percent of these people take their pets on errands at least once a month, says the Yankelovich study. And 28 percent have taken their pets to work. Fifty percent of dogs now sleep in their owners' bedrooms, and half of those sleep on their owners' beds.

This is new territory.

Dogs and people formed bonds thousands of years ago, primarily because the wolflike early dogs offered protection from other predators, Pat Sable wrote in the *National Association of Social Workers Journal* in 1996. Those bonds have evolved so that dogs and people now have intimate emotional connections, Sable observes. Pet therapy, for instance, has grown increasingly popular and successful for cancer patients and others in precarious health; the presence of dogs is said to lessen patients' fears, despair, and sense of isolation.

But beyond the seriously ill, Sable found, dogs are doing more psychological work in the broader population than they've been credited with, helping people through alienation, bereavement, anxiety, and depression. Medical literature, she cautioned, pays too little attention to the psychological role of pets, whose presence "increases feelings of happiness, security and self-worth and reduces feelings of loneliness and isolation."

How to demonstrate such connections? Sable reprinted the results of a questionnaire, first published in *Journal of Marriage and Family* in 1988; written by A. Albert and K. Bulcroft, it was designed to measure the bonds between family members and pets.

The point of the survey, Sable noted, was to learn whether pets are widely considered important family members. They are, the survey found, with dogs the favorite, followed by cats. Where the original questions left a blank (for "pet's name"), I've inserted "Jake." See if the sentiments being tested sound familiar.

1. I feel closer to Jake than to many of my friends.
2. I like Jake because he/she accepts me no matter what I do.
3. Jake makes me feel loved.
4. Jake gives me something to talk about with others.
5. I feel closer to Jake than to other family members.
6. Jake keeps me from being lonely.
7. I like Jake because he/she is more loyal than other people in my life.

16

8. Jake gives me something to take care of.
9. There are times when Jake is my closest companion.

Pet attachment was particularly important, Albert and Bulcroft found, among single, divorced, and widowed people, followed, first, by childless couples, and next by newlyweds and empty-nesters.

Since pets both give and receive affection, they come to function as emotional substitutes, helping to maintain morale when people struggle through transitions. In a society where people often live away from their extended families, watch more and more TV, hook up to cable and the Net, and feel increasingly isolated, where adjustments to new technologies and disruptions of workplaces and relationships characterize modern life—dogs have a lot of new work to do.

There is nothing wrong with forming a powerful attachment to a dog. Loving a dog is often a rich, healthy, incalculably rewarding experience. Nor is it inherently disturbing for people to address or respond to significant emotional issues through their pets. To recognize this behavior isn't to condemn it. Attachment isn't pathological; it's a critical element of human—and interspecies—relationships.

But it *is* important to grasp the truth of our relationship with dogs, for their sakes and ours. We need to understand more about what we are asking them to do and why. Failing to do that can put dogs, and our relationships with them, at risk. If we ask too much of them, they will suffer. We will become disenchanted with them and, in some cases, fail to get the kind of help we really need.

This new kind of work for dogs abounds in Montclair. A dog keeps an ailing, aging man company. Another helps a kid in a poor neighborhood hold his ground and hold on to his pride, but at an awful price. Dogs ease a group of angry, funny women through painful divorces. A woman dying of cancer finds a dog to accompany her through the end of life with joy and affection. A lawyer who, in late middle age, doesn't quite know how to talk to his family, has a best friend to walk with.

These stories offer evidence that the new work of dogs is evolving dramatically, both for people and for dogs.

Sometimes, human-dog relationships are simple, unrelated to the emotional lives and histories of either species. But often, people acquire and love dogs with little awareness that they might have complex and revealing reasons for choosing the pet they choose, loving it the way they do.

Though it can be obvious from the outside, they sometimes don't recognize—and don't necessarily want to recognize—that they're replaying old issues in their own lives through their dogs. Whether this is worthy or appropriate work for dogs to be doing is a question we've given surprisingly little thought to. But some observers have seen trouble coming for a while.

In 1983, psychologist Ralph Slovenko wrote in the journal *Medicine and Law* that pets were increasingly being used to unite families, curb loneliness, help amuse and occupy children, reduce conflict and increase play in family life. They were becoming regarded as something more than animals; they were members of the family. The pet, he wrote, had moved from the backyard to the bedroom.

But if the trend accelerated, he cautioned, it would come at a price. Man is "drastically bending the nature of animals," rarely allowing them outside to roam, altering and/or denying their sexuality.

The domestic dog population, he warned, was even then becoming "obese like their masters, with the health of many in imminent danger." Slovenko in fact quoted a Humane Society official: "We are unwittingly, but relentlessly, turning animals into neurotics."

Almost two decades later, in 2001, the Humane Society reported that nearly 400,000 children under fourteen were bitten seriously enough by dogs to require hospital care, with more than 4 million dog bites reported to doctors and police—evidence that the price Slovenko worried about is indeed being paid. And nobody can say how many minor "nips" and bites simply go unreported.

Dogs are paying for their new work in other ways as well. A vet in a clinic just outside Montclair took me inside a "critical care" room in the back of the office where four dogs lay motionless, attached to respirators and other life-support systems. A fourteen-year-old golden retriever whose cancer had spread to her brain had been comatose for nearly two weeks. Her owner was so emotionally attached to the dog that she refused to euthanize her despite the vet's pleas, arguing that the dog meant too much to her.

"This is now the worst part of my practice," the vet confided, near tears. "I am here to save animals, not torture them."

In 1995, a team of Hungarian researchers conducted one of the few modern studies on how the evolving dog-human relationship can affect dogs' intelligence and problem-solving abilities. We may be dumbing our dogs down.

They found that companion dogs, especially those anthropomorphized by their owners—that is, having human emotions and traits attributed to them—become increasingly dependent. Over time, their abilities to solve problems actually decreased. Not surprising: Dogs are rarely permitted to solve problems. Sheep-herding instructors are forever asking handlers to remain quiet when their dogs are confronted with unexpected situations—sheep running in several directions at once, say—to give the dogs a chance to figure out what to do. But few dogs in contemporary American life, especially those seen as intimate members of a family, get that opportunity. They look to humans for direction.

Sometimes—as with the elderly, the lonely, the disabled, or with some troubled children—the benefits of this redefined relationship are enormous. In other cases, it's not so clear.

I believe that attachment theory offers an important way to help understand and partly explain this increasingly complex turf. As Debra Katz pointed out in her first eye-opening e-mail to me, it's a widely respected and studied view of early childhood and human relationships, first articulated by John Bowlby in his landmark work *Attachment*, published in 1969. Bowlby's focus on attachment relationships shocked and mesmerized developmentalists, psychiatrists, and psychotherapists. Bowlby would eventually stand alongside Freud, Darwin, and Lorenz in "redefining the role of the person in his social context," notes British psychiatrist Peter Fonagy in his book *Attachment Theory and Psychoanalysis*.

The way an infant attaches to and separates from its primary caretaker, its mother, is at the heart of attachment theory. When an infant needs its mother and she is unavailable, the infant becomes extremely agitated and distracted, or protests by getting angry or crying. If it keeps looking for its mother in order to be soothed and can't locate her, the baby eventually enters what some therapists call a state of defensive disregard toward the mother, even when she returns.

Such a child might have problems dealing with complex or stressful situations, since she doesn't really know how to soothe herself. Though the beginnings of the attachment process can be spotted in the earliest weeks of life, it's most evident between four and six months of age, Bowlby wrote.

But its patterns can continue throughout life. This early attachment history shapes the way people regulate their emotions and relate to other people (and, in many cases, to their dogs). When it goes awry, they can suffer difficulties and consequences, to varying degrees, for the rest of their days. Lack of secure attachment is often related to emotional disturbances, anxiety and depression, and problems with relationships.

Psychiatrists have identified four types of childhood attachment and associated behavior traits. They speak of secure children who are confident, who freely explore their environments, and who respond resilently to stress and crisis; and of avoidant children, whose mothers either couldn't or wouldn't respond to their emotional needs. These latter children feel they have to manage on their own, and avoid expressing feelings. They appear somber and self-contained, and can behave dismissively toward their parents and angrily with other children. They've learned not to expect much from others.

Anxious-ambivalent children have primary care-takers who respond to them in insensitive or inconsistent ways. As a result, they become anxious, distressed, and angry; they expect frustration.

Disorganized-disoriented kids show contradictory behaviors, particularly when reunited with their primary caretakers. Alarmed or frightened by a parent's strong emotions, they see their mothers and fathers as a source of both distress and comfort.

Attachment theory's primary contribution is its focus on the infant's need for an unbroken early bond and the impact that has on all future relationships, observes Peter Fonagy. The child who lacks such an attachment is likely to show signs of partial deprivation (an excessive need for love or for revenge, along with guilt and depression); or complete deprivation, characterized by listlessness, quiet unresponsiveness, retarded development; or, later in life, an inability to feel or show emotion, a lack of concentration, patterns of deceit, even compulsive thieving.

What does this have to do with dogs?

A lot, I'd argue. Though some people get dogs for the simplest reasons—hunting, say, or protection—attachment theory helps explain why so many other people get dogs, and how they treat them. It also goes a long way toward illuminating the growing tendency of dog owners to ascribe human characteristics to their animals' behavior. And since dogs, like humans, are creatures that bond with other creatures, attachment theory might help us learn some things about them, as well.

To develop this idea, I learned more about the lives of people and dogs in and around the town of Montclair and entered their homes, vets' offices, training schools, pet stores, yards, parks, and neighborhoods. I also turned to what is, for me, a daunting source: academics and their journals.

I was pleasantly surprised. A number of gifted and articulate researchers were miles ahead of me, and their work and insights laid the groundwork and guided the way, more than I could have imagined.

Psychologist John Archer, for instance, writing in the journal *Evolution and Human Behavior* in 1997, argued that while attachment theory grew from research into children's ties with parents, it applied to pets as well. "There is convincing evidence that people usually view their relationship with pets as similar to those they have with children," he wrote. Pet owners treat pets like children, for example, playing with them, talking to them in "motherese" or baby talk, "continually referring to 'my baby' and holding and cuddling them as one would a baby." He saw evidence that pets can also become parent or partner substitutes.

People often choose dogs because they perceive them as being loving in a particular way they want or need, or needy in ways they can relate to, or forgiving. A man might see a dog as his best friend because his father was cold and distant. A dog owner might find disciplining a dog impossible because he was brutally or cruelly disciplined and now can't bear to be critical himself; he is reworking his own attachment issues by creating a perfectly loving world for his dog. People who felt unloved sometimes need to view their dogs as unconditionally loving. Some people can't bear to neuter their animals, even when appropriate, and others can't deny them endless food or treats.

People who felt mistreated or abandoned may seek to rewrite their own histories by rescuing, in rare cases even hoarding, dogs. Rescue compulsions and fantasies are recognized disorders treated by therapists. So are animal fantasies, in which lonely children and adults search for faithful love and unswerving devotion.

What researchers and therapists are finding—and what dog trainers have intuitively known—is that there *is* a real connection between human attachment issues (especially as people move through life's transitions) and the intensifying evolution of dogs into emotional figures or surrogates.

Animal ethicist James A. Serpell of the University of Pennsylvania, writing in the journal *Applied Animal Behavior Science* in 1996, found a clear though little-studied correlation between companion animal behavior and owner attachment issues. To learn more about it, he said, would be relevant "to our understanding of the potential benefits of pet ownership, and the problems associated with pet loss, or the premature abandonment and disposal of companion animals."

I would like to contribute to that understanding; but in the process of researching this book, I've realized that I have plenty of stories and lots of questions, but far less in the way of clear answers.

Ralph Slovenko was prescient: the relentless anthropomorphizing of dogs in ways that are sometimes wonderful, sometimes disturbing and exploitive, is driving many animals crazy. Apart from the rise in dog bites and other aggressive and neurotic behaviors, the millions of dogs abandoned annually are, in part, a testament to the harm done by humans' misconceptions and misplaced expectations.

There are, sadly, lots of needy, lonely, unfulfilled, and disconnected people. They can perceive in their dogs any trait or emotion they like, unencumbered by the dogs' own voices or those of others who can speak for them. Look how wildly our perceptions of dogs vary, how often they bear little relationship to reality.

At one extreme we hear horror stories, like the recent San Francisco case in which a woman was mauled and killed outside her apartment by her neighbors' two dogs. At the other, we cling to heroic and simplistic images of the Disney dog, of Old Yeller, of Lassie herself—brave, brilliant, and selfless, so loyal that she'd crawl fifty miles through a forest fire to get home.

People who know dogs, and know that they're wonderful but not usually in those ways, shake their heads at such reports. They know that hardly any dog will willfully kill a human unless deliberately trained to, and that hardly any dog will bother to find its way home across huge distances. Most will look for something to eat, then start snuggling up to the human who provided it.

I once told a dog trainer that my dog loved me so single-mindedly that if anything ever happened to me, the dog would probably pine away; he was so loyal that he could never adjust to a new owner. The trainer laughed and said that given two pounds of beef liver and a couple of days, my dog would forget that I ever walked the earth. A friend told me he loved the comforting way his dog licked the blood from his cut while they were out hiking. How caring. But dogs are predators; they love fresh blood, from almost any source.

Both the life-threatening and the heroic dog, despite the enormous volume of media coverage, are statistically aberrant, to say the least. They have as much to do with the average dog or human as a moon launch has with a bike ride.

Our real-life dramas tend to be intense but mundane: unemployment, divorce, illness, loneliness, fear, abandonment. This seems to be the kind of work dogs can sometimes actually handle.

Harried and distracted as our everyday lives have

become, it's possible that we are living through a great change in the historic relationship between dogs and humans, while many of us don't really notice or think much about it. We bring animals into our homes to live among our families, and now we ask them to do much more than sit and fetch. Yet we often have little comprehension of why we feel about them as we do.

Why do people love their dogs?

Evidence of this affection is ancient: fossils show a relationship between humans and wolflike canines half a million years ago. The domestication of dogs apparently dates back at least 12,000 years, when a puppy was buried in the Middle East in a coffin with a human, who was positioned with his hand around the dog.

But dog ownership is puzzling in a Darwinian sense, because it seems so one-sided: we feed and shelter them, but what, precisely, do they do for us? So many other animal species are dying off, suffering from human greed, cruelty, or mere lack of interest; why are we so devoted to this one?

Psychologist John Archer considers three explanations for humans' love of dogs. One is that strong feelings toward a pet indicate some inadequacy in a person's human relationships, though he notes that many scholars vehemently disagree, and he concludes that the love of dogs is too widespread to be viewed as abnormal or neurotic.

Beneficial consequences for both species are

another possible explanation. Dog-keeping, one sociologist writes, "is genuinely adaptive in the evolutionary sense of the word, since it contributes to individual health and survival by ameliorating the stresses and strains of everyday life. These benefits far outweigh the costs of caring for the animal."

In fact, pet owners show significantly reduced risks of heart disease and high blood pressure, says one American Medical Association study. They exercise more than non-pet owners, and on average they live a year longer.

But the reason that Archer thinks comes closest to the truth is that dogs are social parasites in the best, most adaptive sense of the term—able to insert themselves into the social system of another species in order not only to survive but to sleep on soft beds and get great stuff to eat. Because dogs clearly have *some* emotions—love, fear, arousal, sexual feelings—humans assume they have many more. For their part, dogs have learned, with Nature's help, to trigger our emotional responses, so that we will have strong feelings for them.

Despite a dog's limited intellect and language, owners often behave as if their dogs can understand and respond to them. Archer cites a survey of visitors to veterinary clinics, of whom nearly 80 percent acknowledged that they talked to their animals as if they were human; an equal proportion believed their pets were sensitive to their feelings. Psychologists call this human tendency "the theory of mind," the willingness to attribute complex feelings and thoughts to other people, animals, or objects.

For the most part, dogs have managed to avoid those judgemental or confrontational elements that make human relationships so complicated. As one respondent to a dog study put it, "They love me even without makeup." Humans love their dogs, Archer concludes, because they manipulate us so skillfully.

Last year, a team led by Harvard biological anthropologist Brian Hare found that dogs demonstrate an uncanny ability—far better than our closer relative, the chimpanzee—to read human cues and behavior, accurately interpreting even subtle hand gestures and glances. Hare and his fellow researchers found that this talent has become an innate trait among dogs, selected and bred over thousands of years to live compatibly with humans.

But as earlier research and that unhappy vet's critical-care room demonstrate, such manipulative ability may backfire. It's not always good news for dogs.

Are we asking more of them than any animal can give? Projecting more thoughts and feelings than they can possibly have, and sometimes turning on them when they can't deliver? Are we sometimes using dogs to hide from problems? Are we treating dogs as we wish *we* were treated or as they need to be treated? More simply, are we allowing our dogs to be dogs?

And what does this new work of dogs say about us and our society?

The world of dog owners has its share of hierarchies and subcultures, among them a sometimes smug group who believe that the only real working dogs are the storied border collies, shepherds, hounds, and retrievers bred to herd livestock or hunt game—work rather few of them ever get to do nowadays, anyway.

But if there's a single conclusion emerging from my years of hanging around with dogs and people, it's this: all dogs are working dogs. Nearly every breed—even lap dogs—were developed for specific tasks. Every dog is descended from creatures who aided primitive, frightened humans when they most needed it. Today, when we are less primitive but still frightened, they are working harder than ever.

CHAPTER 2

THE GOOD MOTHER

Sandra Robinson was forty-one when I first met her on a bitter-cold night three days before Christmas Eve. She came to the door to let me into the modest house where she was renting the first-floor apartment. An attractive, slightly stocky woman in a loose-fitting shaggy sweater and pants, she wore her tangle of short dirty-blond hair just above her shoulders. She had a funny, self-deprecating air, apologizing for her apartment, for the way she looked, and for the fact that she was very—*very*—excited.

Two days earlier she had driven to a breeder in Delaware and returned with a dachshund puppy she named Eleanor Rigby.

A tiny ball of brown fur barely eight inches long, the dog now lay curled up dozing in the corner of a used crib in the dining room. The crib, filled with strips of newspaper, chew toys, and micro-treats for small dogs, was where Ellie would sleep, at least until she was housebroken. On the windowsill nearby, a small green plastic tree with blinking lights faced onto the street.

Christmas could be a tough time for single people in family-centered towns like Montclair. Homes and shops festooned with wreaths and lights. A mad scramble for last-minute toys at malls and downtown stores. Christmas tree marts sprouting in vacant lots. Crowds headed for school holiday performances and parties all over town.

Sandra had been feeling excluded from all the festivities—"on the outside of this bright and colorful circle," she told me as she sat down on the sofa. But that, she added philosophically, came with "this life." She meant the life of an unhappy single woman, discontented with work, recently divorced, disappointed with the results of serial dating, all this Christmas cheer coming at a time when she was slowly and painfully giving up on the idea of finding a good man. Instead, she said, she'd opted for a good dog.

So far, she was delighted. "With Ellie here, I already feel more a part of it," she said. "I've got a family, too. And the best Christmas present I've ever gotten. Figures I bought it for myself."

A refugee from Manhattan, Sandra had been in the apartment for three months now. The interior was spartan, with plain white curtains and furnishings so nondescript that the interior could've been depicted in an Edward Hopper painting. It smelled slightly of litter box. Sandy explained she also had a twelve-year-old cat who would make it a point to stay out of sight; she'd been pouting ever since Ellie arrived.

Perhaps the apartment had come furnished; it felt that impersonal, with no framed photographs, no antiques or artwork, none of the bric-a-brac indicating that someone had lived here for a while or planned to stay. This wasn't a woman to whom material objects mattered, which was just as well. Being somewhat unfastidious is a necessary trait for dog people, who learn to overlook a lot of smells, stains, and hair. As much as dogs' roles may have evolved, many of their personal habits still date to the Stone Age. But a puppy couldn't do too much damage here.

"Ellie loves her," Sandra was saying of Tia, the cat. "She wants to be friends, you can see it. But Tia's having none of it."

Sandra had skipped over social amenities like inviting her guest to sit down or offering a drink, as if she were done with that sort of thing, tired perhaps of waiting on men, or even having one around. The subject seemed to exhaust her.

Every few minutes, her personality shifted a bit: friendly but wary, open but cautious, needy but buttoned-up. She admitted to feeling somewhat disoriented, a single professional living in a charmless flat in a working-class section of a town so centered around schools and kids and family life.

Why had she come here?

"New York. It was just defeating me," she said. She'd heard that Montclair had lots of movie theaters, restaurants, an art museum. Perhaps one day she could buy a house, maybe meet somebody and marry again, although "I am coming to terms with the fact that that probably is not going to happen. A big point in the life of any woman."

But she'd have things to do here, and the rents would be saner, the pace a bit less frenzied. And Manhattan a mere sixteen miles away. Her best friend Zoe, another woman whose original plans hadn't quite materialized and who found herself in the unexpected situation of delivering priority mail for the U.S. Postal Service, lived nearby.

Most of the year, Sandra maintained, she thought she'd like living in a child-oriented place, even if she didn't have a child herself. Besides, her new landlord had agreed that she could have a small dog.

Ellie stirred in the crib and Sandra stood up quickly, walked over, and picked her up. Ellie squirmed happily as Sandra brought her over to the couch, where Ellie curled up in her lap and went back to sleep. The dog was tiny, her dominant feature her enormous, expressive brown eyes. Sandra relaxed visibly, growing more peaceful, nearly glowing with affection.

Not even the dog's peeing in her lap upset her. "Oh, my baby, you had to go," she cooed, depositing Ellie back in the crib while she went into the bedroom to change her pants. Referring to their dogs as babies, cuddling and holding them as if they actually were—shrinks call this "motherese."

35

"Sorry," Sandra said, emerging. "I'll have to take her out and housebreak her soon, I guess, but it's so cold out and she seems so little and fragile." Soon, Ellie was resettled in Sandra's lap and Sandra was stroking her contentedly.

She had been through a hellish couple of years, it turned out. She'd been living with her second husband in a one-bedroom apartment on the Lower East Side, with hundreds of restaurants, clubs, and theaters a few blocks away. She'd lived in the city for years, since graduating from NYU with a business degree.

She and her husband had just agreed to a no-fault divorce after a four-year marriage both of them understood to have been a mistake almost from the start.

"Four *long* years," she was saying. They met through the personal ads in *New York* magazine, "but we were Mars and Venus, two distant planets who happened to be thrown together. Both of us were lonely. But I love theater and movies, he loves sports. I love going out, he hates going out. My family was a nightmare, his was out of Norman Rockwell. I was aching to have a kid, he wasn't sure he ever wanted one. Why didn't we talk about this first? Because I'm just dumb about these things. And, oh yes, I love my cat Tia and he hates cats. There wasn't a thing we shared."

There had been an earlier marriage that was apparently even worse and which she didn't want to say much about. "I married my father, as they say," she volunteered, staring at her blinking tree. "A brutish, sadistic drunk who took off." Sandra had a way of shaking her head as she told these stories, a how-on-earth-could-I-be-that-dumb gesture. Her life had been filled with disappointments, it seemed, some of them deeper than she first admitted.

She and her second husband had both ridden the Internet mania of the 1990s for a while, on the way up and on the way down, working for dot-coms in various capacities from writing to design. But even when times were good, she hated her Web designer job, the long hours, the ambitious and demanding bosses, the fact that everybody she worked with was barely of voting age and had no interests outside a computer screen. It wasn't the first or last time I was to hear a dog owner talk about how unhappy she was at work.

The marriage dissolved quickly, amicably; they hadn't talked since, but she wished him well. "The funny thing was, we never even had a fight. It was bloodless. One night at dinner we both agreed this hadn't worked out; the next week he was gone. But it was still pretty awful, because by now I've passed forty and my chances for the kind of life I wanted are dwindling."

She got to keep Tia the cat.

The aftermath was tough, though.

A man she began dating some months later was simultaneously courting another woman, something Sandra found out about through a friend. He lied, then admitted it, then vanished. Afterward, one blind date failed to show up at the restaurant, another date grew abusive in a bar, cursing her and calling her a pig, and in the fall she'd gotten laid off.

Two or three months of ensuing depression led to a long visit with her mother in a small Delaware town. "I'm one of those people who lets trouble pile up," she said ruefully. "Then it knocks me over."

Sandra and her mother, an alcoholic, hadn't spoken for years. But her mother had joined AA and stopped drinking. The town had a chapter of Al-Anon, a support group for alcoholics' children; she urged Sandra to go to the meeting, held in a church basement. It shattered her before it helped her, "probably because it was really the first time I faced the reality of my own life."

It was on this visit that a cousin who bred dachshunds offered Sandra a puppy—for $500—from a new litter. "I figured what the hell," she said. "There was absolutely no reliable person in my life except my friend Zoe, and Tia was getting old and cranky. By now I was closing in on forty-two and understood that I had blown my shot at being a mother and wasn't likely to get another one. And I couldn't bear struggling with men anymore. I'd never dealt with the problems of my original family, and here came this stream of other problems. I realized in Al-Anon that I had a lot of issues to face, and hadn't faced any of them, really. I decided to accept reality, give up for the moment, stop looking for people who would only bring me pain, who have rarely failed to disappoint me, and get a dog."

For the next couple of weeks, Sandra and Ellie barely left the apartment. When forced out to the supermarket or the bank, she took the dog along, swathed in blankets on the backseat of the car.

"I was wildly in love from the first," Sandra announced. "This dog is so sweet, I almost can't believe it. I just can't describe to anybody how much I love this dog. I don't have words for it. It's the purest relationship anyone can imagine—all she does is love me." So much that Sandra couldn't bear to leave Ellie, not to go into the city, meet friends, explore her new town, or go to the movies.

Ellie was, in fact, an especially affectionate dog—as dogs tend to be when from puppyhood they are treated lovingly by the same person all day long, plied with food and toys, and have their bellies scratched for hours. Ellie rolled over on her back and practically melted whenever Sandy picked her up or talked to her.

Playful, growling, wrestling with toys and bedding, Ellie loved visitors, too, greeting them eagerly, jumping into their laps to lick their faces. She was the kind of dog few people would shy away from, reliable around strangers, kids, anybody.

If Sandra had momentarily decided to withdraw from people, her dog couldn't get enough of them—an interesting match, and a refutation of the notion that dogs mirror their owners' personalities. Perhaps, as Sandra suggested, Ellie had the personality she herself wanted to have.

What was clear was that the puppy was going to be her once-in-a-lifetime dog, the kind that intersects with someone at a significant, often transitional point: after an illness or a death, or at the end of a marriage.

Sandra's situation—real emotional pain, enormous personal and professional flux, unresolved family issues, a solitary move to a new community without work—was classic.

In her book *Twins* psychoanalyst Dorothy Burlingham describes the deep yearning children and lonely adults have for make-believe animals: "The child takes an imaginary animal as his intimate and beloved companion; subsequently he is never separated from his animal friend, and in this way he overcomes loneliness."

Burlingham's child was very much on my mind as I entered the homes and emotional lives of people and their nonimaginary, beloved dogs all over town. Again and again, a person in difficulty, isolation, or transition was choosing the very kind of dog Burlingham's kid pined for: a creature who understands her loneliness, unhappiness, and need for comfort and support. The animal then offers precisely what Burlingham's child wanted: faithful love, unswerving devotion, uninterrupted availability. There is nothing that the animal can't grasp or intuit. It will not reject or abandon. Speech is not only impossible but unnecessary; understanding comes without words.

From the dog's perspective, of course, less is known. Dogs do respond to love, as well as to cruelty, and the more warmly they're treated, the stronger their own attachments become. They tend toward behaviors that are reinforced, that get humans' attention. They want to please. Beyond that, nobody really knows. But Ellie, having wandered into a powerful human drama, was doing her part effortlessly. Both partners in this pair were enjoying themselves. From the first, though, Sandra understood that there were deeper issues swirling.

On one visit, stroking Ellie's floppy brown ears, I said something about a true love, and Sandra cringed. Later, she told me it was hard to hear. A number of people had pointed out that Ellie seemed to adore Sandra. But it seemed dangerous, even though it was clearly the truth. Relationships were not safe. "I guess I don't really expect love from anyone I come in contact with," she confessed. "I've gone without love so much in my life that I question my ability to attract love—no matter what form it appears in."

It made sense, really. When you love something that much, and are as vulnerable as Sandra, how can you not fear losing it?

The downside, though, was that puppies need

more than love. As is common, even prevalent, among dog owners, Sandra knew shockingly little about dogs when she brought Ellie home. She had no idea what to feed her, what size she would become, what the characteristics of the breed were. She'd never had a dog or been close to anybody else's. She didn't know the most rudimentary training or housebreaking principles.

From the first, Sandra balked at discipline and training, though she heard much about benign training philosophies like positive reinforcement. Weeks later, the dog was still sleeping—and moving its bowels—in the crib, and when I suggested that this might prove a tough habit to break when the dog got older, Sandra shrugged and said she'd deal with that later. She shrugged some more when the vet warned her that she was overfeeding the puppy, which was visibly overweight, even at four months old, because of the ceaseless rain of treats, table food, and kibble she was providing, along with only minimal exercise.

Ellie whimpered when Sandra brought her into her own bed, and sometimes the dog eliminated there. Or on the kitchen floor. Or on the dining room carpet.

Trainers, breeders, and behaviorists uniformly speak of the critical need to train dogs in some intelligent, clear, and positive way. Training not only keeps them safe—away from cars and streets, for instance—but it brings order to their relationship with people, provides them with a notion of place in their social structure, gives shape to their working instincts. It helps them to make sense of their world.

Like kids, dogs need to understand what the rules are so that they can relax, obey them, and feel safe. Natural dog behavior often doesn't mesh with human customs. When dogs don't know the rules, don't understand where to eliminate, what to chew, how to behave, they get into trouble. They grow confused and frightened, they anger or upset the humans they live with, and may develop a wide range of neurotic and aggressive behaviors that make everyone unhappy.

Yet to Sandra, at least initially, training was an unbearable prospect. She couldn't tolerate the thought of spaying Ellie, either, though not spaying her could present a whole range of problems for the dog. She thought Ellie too fragile to endure discipline, too sweet to really need any.

Here's where things get complicated, especially when people see dogs as human-like. Dogs can learn to follow simple rules, but they are not moral creatures. They learn behaviors, not concepts like right or wrong.

They often can't meet all their owners' expectations; they simply can't be sufficiently clean, quiet, understanding, asexual, nonaggressive, or unconditionally loving. When they're not, they are sometimes harshly treated, sometimes abandoned.

Certainly Ellie could not grasp the importance of eliminating outside unless someone taught her.

But it didn't seem likely that Sandra would, at least not anytime soon.

Sometimes she put disposable diapers on the dog. She repeatedly swabbed the crib mattress with Lysol. "I can't even bear to take her outside," she confessed. "It's been so cold, and she's so little, so loving. I just wanted the two of us to be together all the time."

The dog *was* tiny; she still fit comfortably into Sandra's hand and forearm, cradled like a baby. Sandra sat for hours stroking Ellie as she lay dozing in her lap. Occasionally, when Ellie toddled off to sleep on a little dog bed in the corner of the living room, Sandra was wounded, but didn't interfere. "I decided it was her choice," she announced. She'd felt coerced enough in her life; she wasn't about to do that to her dog. "But I have to admit, it hurt. I wanted her to be in my lap all the time. I couldn't get enough of this love."

Meanwhile, she flooded the apartment with squeaky toys, stuffed animals with soundmakers. The fuzz (though some are plastic with no fur) provides the sensation of mouthing a real animal, and the high-pitched noise arouses dogs' prey instincts, the drive to chase and capture. They're perfect diversions for dogs, who are predators after all, and for their owners, who think they're cute.

Sadly, as any dog owner knows, squeaky toys are rather expensive—they can cost from five to twenty-five dollars—and can withstand the average puppy's onslaught for only a day or two. Kids can treasure their stuffed animals for years; active dogs, for hours. But since dogs do come to love them, they sell like mad. Sandra, who was unemployed with little cash to spare, had bought tons of them.

Yet buying a plastic crate for housebreaking or confinement was unthinkable. Her landlord—who lived, by the way, with ten stray cats—insisted that "caging" dogs was inhumane. He didn't have to work hard to persuade Sandra.

"For the first time in my life, I'm getting this kind of raw, pure, completely unconditional love," she explained. "I keep telling myself, God, you can get this even from a different species."

At this point, Sandra seemed to me to be edging past what I'd come to call the "balance point," when attachment to a dog can become unhealthy or problematic. It was an idea I developed while spending time with dozens of people and their dogs. Lots of dog people adore their pets; a few appear to go too far.

Dogs seem to thrive when they are one element in a person's life, balanced against other things—a partner or spouse, kids, compelling work, engaging interests and hobbies, close friendships. As the number of other elements dwindle, the dog's place in an owner's life grows larger, sometimes too large, threatening to shut out much of the world. These, perhaps, are the people who can't take their dogs off respirators and allow them to die, people whose love for their dogs becomes all-consuming.

Children can eventually speak up for themselves, and there are teachers, peers, and relatives to provide their parents some feedback. But there's nothing that mediates between an owner and a dog, no outside perspective.

Sandra kept spraying the apartment with disinfectants until even the landlord, thinking of his property, urged her to take Ellie out for walks. So, though she privately thought it cruel, Sandra bought a leash and started using it.

Once they began walking daily, Sandra was startled by how much they both enjoyed it. For Ellie, there were new sights and sounds, birds and squirrels to watch, interesting smells to linger over, other dogs to greet. More significantly, there were people.

On their walks, Ellie began leading her to other dog owners and people on the block and around town—or so Sandra believed. She described the dachshund as the neighborhood celebrity, adored by children, other dogs, everyone. "She would pull me right across the street if there was a dog nearby. Or even into stores to meet somebody." A barely one-pound dachshund pulling a grown woman across a street? Sandra laughed, blushed, and conceded. "Well, I guess she pulled me where I wanted to go."

A single or childless person in Montclair could easily come to feel invisible. "Nobody talks to you," Sandra had found. "You're shut out of the main life of the place. But when you walk around with a cute and friendly puppy, people line up to talk to you. Almost every stranger you see smiles and comes over."

When she'd felt most withdrawn, a dachshund had brought her back into contact with people. "It was very healing."

Meeting neighbors and dog walkers, she peppered them with questions. How often did they walk their dogs? What did they eat? How were they housebroken?

Sandra was doing some freelance design work from home during this period, living mostly off her savings and a small loan unexpectedly offered by her mother. She was beginning to doubt whether she could ever return to an office, and was considering going back to school. She attributed much of this rethinking to the dog.

"It isn't only that I don't want to leave her all day . . . It's more that she's forced me to think about things, started a process where I am thinking about how to live my life, rather than just to survive it."

Increasingly curious about dogs, she began ordering useful-looking books online, trawling through the pets section in bookstores, asking friends for advice and recommendations. When she went to the pet store, she quizzed the owner about food, treats, training; she bought Ellie vitamin supplements, baked "gourmet" dog treats, hypoallergenic biscuits, even a small—though rarely used—crate for housebreaking.

She started visiting chat rooms and online mailing lists, too, meeting people who were just as smitten as she was. One of them, a computer programmer who lived with three dogs in Morris County, even asked her out.

She froze. She wasn't ready.

Months later, on a steamy summer day, the rest of Sandra's story emerged. The street was eerily quiet, a calm that descends on Montclair when the school buses are garaged, the music lessons are suspended, the minivans sit parked in garages and driveways or are off at the shore.

Ellie was lying on the sofa next to Sandy, who was stroking her. The dog had grown, but she was slimmer than before; Sandra had stopped overfeeding her. And the crib was gone from the adjacent room. Ellie had occasional accidents, but was mostly housebroken, finally. But some things hadn't changed: Sandra was talking about why she loved this dog so much.

As so often happens with dogs, it went way back.

Sandra's father was a sadistic abuser who left when she was eight and hadn't been heard from since, she said. Her mother had rarely been conscious or sober for much of her childhood. But there was more.

Sandra's eyes began to water. She walked into her bedroom and returned with a silver-framed photograph: a young woman with long dark hair holding a baby. "Look, I meant to tell you but I just couldn't until now. I have a daughter. In fact, I have a granddaughter."

It took several visits before Sandra could tell the whole story, or talk about it comfortably. At seventeen, she'd become pregnant. Her mother, a Catholic who didn't believe in abortion, insisted that Sandra give birth, but she also told her, "Of course, you're in no position to raise it." So Sandra placed the child for adoption and never made a subsequent effort to contact her.

Yet she'd thought about her daughter every day of her life, she told me soberly, and agonized about whether to seek her out or not. The debate continued until she was thirty-six, when she tracked her daughter down in Philadelphia. Her child, already married and already a mother, announced that she hated Sandra and wanted nothing to do with her.

They eventually did meet and speak, several times. But their relationship was difficult, even hostile, for which Sandra blamed only herself. She was trying to accept that things might never get any better. Yet another cycle of loss and pain. She stopped calling.

"At Al-Anon, they teach you not to phone pain," she said, "which means, don't seek out people who cause you suffering. When my daughter is ready, she knows where to find me and I'll do everything I can to have a relationship with her. Until then . . ." She left the sentence unfinished and sat quietly, stroking the dachshund.

"My daughter hasn't begun to deal with what I did to her," she said after a while. "And I haven't begun to forgive myself."

Still, what was happening to her was dizzying. She had given up on being a mother, but suddenly her own mother had reentered her life. So had her biological daughter, however glancingly, and now *she* was a mother—so Sandra found herself a grandmother to a child she might never know through a daughter she might never be able to communicate with. And then there was Ellie.

"All of a sudden," Sandra told me later, "I could be a mommy. Did I understand that this need related to my own history, my own situation? Of course. I'm not stupid. But people called me 'Ellie's mom' every time we went out. I can't tell you how much I love that, how much that means to me. Finally, I got to be a good mother."

On the sofa, Ellie rolled over, hopped onto the floor, and pounced on one of her squeaky toys. We watched her play.

"Last month, my cat Tia died," Sandra said. "I'd had that cat for twelve years. When I got home from the vet, I couldn't stop crying. Ellie licked my tears away. I sat there sobbing for two hours and she sat right with me. What can I say? I know she's a dog, not a person. But relationships are hard, and sometimes it's just easier to let them go."

Especially when you have a different kind of dependent in the house, one that will never resent you, demand explanations, or withhold forgiveness.

Sandra had begun contacting potential employers, considering a new career as a marketer for rural craftspeople trying to reach urban consumers via the Net. Her story seemed to be edging toward a more promising, less painful, chapter. Ellie had done her work—if not consciously, then well.

But these two were lucky. Ellie was a tiny, easygoing dog who didn't need a lot of exercise or show much working instinct or hunting drive. And Sandra's excesses tended to be affectionate, not neglectful or threatening.

She still found it unbearable sometimes to discipline Ellie, who jumped and barked repeatedly for attention whenever Sandra was working at the computer. "She just wants me to play with her," Sandra said apologetically, as if that made it okay. She could not bring herself to train the dog to lie down or back off, or even to put Ellie in her crate when she was obnoxious. So e-mailing or working online was marked by constant barking and interruptions. Eventually, Sandra ignored her, a tactic that began to work.

If Ellie were bigger and more rambunctious, if Sandra hadn't been home and available to provide such affection and attention, their relationship could easily have turned out very differently, as anyone working in a shelter could attest.

Another dog—confined, overfed, underexercised,

untrained—could have grown neurotic or aggressive, capable of much worse destruction than the occasional carpet stain. That, in turn, could have provoked a different owner to anger, and a much different outcome.

Outside, taking a walk around the block on a summer day, Ellie was, sure enough, on the lookout for neighbors and passersby, tugging Sandra toward them, accepting the exclamations—"So cuuuuute" and "Pupp-ee!"—from all sides. Maybe she sensed Sandra's pleasure in meeting people this way, or maybe she simply approached people instinctively. But nobody passed whom Ellie didn't try to greet, tail going. Many people seemed to know Sandra and Ellie, greeting them by name, chatting.

It was like watching a candidate on the campaign trail. This might not have been the picture of a balanced, fulfilled life, and there were still problems—Ellie had suddenly become aggressive with large dogs, for example. But it wasn't a portrait of isolation and misery either.

Two nights earlier, Sandra told me as we strolled back to her apartment that she had finally agreed, after many invitations, to meet the programmer in Morristown. She left Ellie in the crate she'd bought at the pet store—the dog didn't seem to mind at all—stocking it with enough treats, toys, and chew bones for a two-week stay.

Approaching the agreed-on restaurant, she saw her prospective date sitting alone, in khakis and a green shirt, just as he'd said. She took in his balding head and squat torso and started to bolt.

"But then I thought, no, this is wrong. Do I really want my dog to be more friendly than I am? I thought of Ellie's openness and how she trusts everyone, and I thought, this is an example. I need to take chances, be as trusting as she is.

"So I went in. And we had a nice time. He loves his dogs the way I love my dog. We spent three hours talking and are going to get together again. He's coming over next week to meet Ellie."

CHAPTER 3

SAINT BETTY JEAN

"There they are," said Betty Jean Scirro, spotting the two familiar minivans idling at the end of a row behind a pet shop in nearby Wayne, New Jersey. It was just before sunrise on a cold, rainy Sunday in early November.

The scene was almost, by Jersey standards, pastoral. The humming highway was nearly quiet, and the usually jammed lot was empty. Misty puffs of breath rose from the tiny knot of people standing by the vans.

Betty Jean's dog rescue group, Save the Pets, Inc., was planning one of its regular assaults on a municipal animal shelter in Brooklyn. The idea was to pull some dogs out and ferry them to safe houses in Montclair before the shelter could put them to sleep.

The transport vehicles were fitting. A minivan can transport three or four crates at a time; it's reasonably safe in case of an accident, and it's much cheaper and less gas-guzzling than a big SUV. Dog rescue people tend to have continuous expenses and little cash; they'd prefer to put their money into rescue, not gasoline.

Rescue people are the Special Forces of the dog world—fearless, driven, intensely organized, wily and resourceful, unstoppable, unwavering in the righteousness of their cause.

The very notion of "dog rescue" is uniquely American—a suddenly massive, technologically driven new subculture. Animal shelters have been around for more than a century, along with people willing to adopt unwanted dogs. But in the late 1980s and early nineties, as the number of dogs in America was soaring, so was the number of abandoned and unwanted dogs overwhelming shelters' capacities and being euthanized.

With the Internet and the easily linked and suddenly accessible sites of the World Wide Web, the idea of dog rescue took off. Type "dog rescue" into the Internet search engine called Google and more than 700,000 references pop up. Rescue groups have formed for almost every breed in almost every city and state, some with scores of members, fund-raising campaigns, sometimes even their own vans, caps, jackets, badges, and bumper stickers. For the first time, rescuers and potential adopters are able to communicate via a network of sites and mailing lists.

Dog rescue groups, nearly all operated by volunteers, go almost entirely unregulated, occupying something of a gray zone. Many work closely with animal shelters, but some have an uneasy, even hostile relationship with civic officials and shelters responsible for animal welfare. Ovewhelmed and underfunded public facilities wind up killing dogs as well as finding homes for them; rescue groups work feverishly to save them. That sometimes creates tension between a bureaucracy bound by wildly varying ordinances and few resources and a growing army of dog-loving individualists.

Betty Jean's organization, along with many in and around Montclair, posts its listings on its website and on sites like Petfinder.com (www.petfinder.com), one of the biggest Internet clearinghouses for rescue groups and rescued dogs. On this fall day, Petfinder had nearly 100,000 "adoptable pets" on its website, allowing potential pet owners across the country to search through databases for the kind of dog or cat they wanted. Often, rescue groups work together to transport dogs hundreds of miles to new homes. In theory, every dog in need of a home can now go anywhere, and any person wanting a dog can scour the country in seconds.

Betty Jean was legendary in these circles, a pioneer, role model, inspiration, and rallying point. Everyone in dog rescue around New Jersey had heard of her. Her worshipful troops described her as selfless, tireless, and effective. People called and visited her from all over the country to see how it should be done.

She'd risen at four A.M. to prepare for this trip, but even so, she'd had barely enough time to attend to all the tasks she had to do this and every morning before she could think of leaving her house.

Betty Jean had lived for thirty-five years in a classic northern New Jersey split-level, built during the great boom when tract houses engulfed the northeastern corner of the state, where broad interstates bisected neighborhoods and towns and the words "New Jersey" and "ugly" became forever synonymous in the national consciousness.

Most of Montclair was built well before then, and the town prided itself on the beauty of its surviving architecture, but parts of its borders looked much like the newer suburbs that surrounded it.

Betty Jean wouldn't disclose her age, but she admitted to being a couple of years away from Social Security checks. She lived alone, if you could say that about her actually very crowded house. Her husband left years ago—she hadn't spoken to him once since—her kids were grown, and she discouraged visits from the grandchildren. Although she had an "office job," she hated every minute of it and rarely spoke of it. It simply provided the means for her to cover her own bills and pay for the group's dog supplies, plus phone and vet expenses. Her salary didn't go very far.

No one at her job knew she was involved with rescue; but, then, no one next door did either. Even her longtime neighbors thought she was just another dog nut.

Yet rescue was her life, her real work, family, and purpose; nothing else came close. Her dream was to leave clerical work behind and raise just enough money—about $20,000 a year would do it, she figured, along with her pension and Social Security—to devote herself to rescue work full-time. In the same way writers, artists, and actors fantasized about giving up their day jobs to pursue their passions, dog rescuers plotted how to do nothing but save dogs. And there were plenty to save.

Betty Jean didn't like to ask people for money, but members of her group had been collecting pledges for a couple of years to underwrite her future. So far they had $9,000 pledged, but no hard cash in the bank.

Apart from the wooden cats that graced the front lawn, there was nothing to distinguish Betty Jean's green-shingled house from the many like it—until you went inside.

The doorbell's ring set off a brief torrent of barking. Betty Jean opened the door slowly, cautiously, with steady injunctions to be careful and move slowly.

She was tiny, a bit over five feet tall, and so thin as to appear birdlike, her hair tinted a pale red. She looked weary. Even at that hour, though, there was a twinkle of mischief in her eyes. She was wearing slippers and a blue fleece bathrobe, apologizing for not yet having found time to dress.

She sized up her visitor in a practiced way and got down to business, no time for chitchat.

"Watch the little white one," she muttered, as a scrappy white terrier circled. "He's a boarder, and he likes to bite ankles." Betty Jean's home, it soon became clear, was one you entered at your own risk. The terrier dove at my shoes, snarling, until Betty Jean scolded him away. She took in boarder

58

dogs, she explained, to help cover the costs of rescue.

What was one more dog? There were already twenty-two housed in her playroom and the adjacent garage; a glass wall had been installed between them, allowing each room to be visible from the other.

Before Betty Jean could head out for Brooklyn, which she did once or twice a week, she had to feed all twenty-two and let them outside—along with several cats and her own five dogs—while settling the squabbles that inevitably erupted over territory, attention, food, and toys.

It promised to be a busy morning. Six puppies with mange required special medication administered with a dropper, plus fresh dog bedding—towels, old quilts, and blankets—laundered and changed twice a day.

One or two "problem" dogs, big, aggressive animals fresh from the streets of Brooklyn via the shelter, were apt to attack other dogs or threaten people and needed intense socialization and attention. Some required years of work before they were deemed trustworthy and adoptable. Some would come back, too much for their new owners. Some would never be adopted, Betty Jean conceded on rare occasions. But such dogs held a special place in the hearts of rescue people; they were the neediest of the needy, the last to be adopted, the first to be euthanized at a shelter. So here they were at Betty Jean's halfway house.

Meanwhile, four or perhaps five cats (she hadn't seen the shy one for a week or so) were skittering about, hopping up onto tabletops, yowling for food.

The exact maneuvers by which Betty Jean moved the dogs out of their crates, into her fenced yard, and then back again were an impressive blur. It was almost as if she set them moving so rapidly, keeping them confused about what they were doing, that they forgot to cause trouble.

All of this had to be accomplished efficiently and silently, so as not to alert or annoy her neighbors, whose patience was sometimes sorely tested. "I clean out the poop fifty times a day. I stay on top of that. Mostly, they complain about urine smells from the backyard," she sighed. "I pour gallons of disinfectant and bleach out there. And I have to control the noise. Any dog that's barky goes to another member of the group."

It was fascinating to see what Betty Jean, a study in multi-tasking, could accomplish in mere minutes. A crate opens; a dog gets shooed out into the yard as another darts back inside. The puppies are let loose in the playroom to squeal and chase one another while Betty Jean speedily changes their bedding, tosses soaked and soiled newspapers into a special trash bin, hurriedly applies droppers of medication, hides pills in food or—a last resort—rams them down the dogs' throats.

She got dressed in stages, letting a few dogs out,

pulling on pants and a shirt, letting dogs in, fussing with her hair, feeding the cats, then applying a bit of makeup.

She fed the big dogs all at once to minimize the excitement and forestall the inevitable protests and complaining, grabbing a ripped forty-pound bag of kibble donated by a pet store, filling bowls, opening the crates, blocking the exits, shoving the bowls inside, keeping up a string of exhortations. "You stay where you are, young man." And "Don't be a bad girl now. I *mean* it."

An enormous, menacing-looking rottweiler mother pushed out of one crate, looking anxiously for her two pups down the row.

Betty Jean, who knew better, suddenly found herself between the mom and her babies, a place she didn't want to be. The rottweiler was already agitated; the family had been transported from a city shelter a day earlier, just hours before the mother was to be put down. The shelter's paperwork labeled her dangerous and a biter—they put what they call a "caution" on her—but that meant little. "She might have just been protecting her pups," Betty Jean said.

Besides, she mistrusted shelters' evaluations: "I take my own look," she announced. "I make my own decisions." Rottweilers and pit bulls might arouse fear and concern among the general population, but rescue people had a soft spot for them, because they were often in the most urgent need of rescue. Aware of the bad publicity and ugly stereotyping a few such dogs generated, they countered with an endless stream of tales about pit bulls and rotties that had been turned around, how loving they were by nature, what great pets they made.

Just now Betty Jean was in too much of a hurry to risk getting bitten. "You," she barked, holding her hand up to the growling mother. "Knock it off. Get back into your crate. I've got too much to do. You'll see your girls later, I promise. They're okay. Get back in there." Betty Jean moved behind the mother and urged her back into the crate, alternately soothing and scolding.

A minute later, a giant shepherd mix came charging in. "Quick, behind the door," Betty Jean yelled. I dove for the sliding glass door separating the two rooms as a huge shepherd, weighing easily eighty pounds, slammed into the glass. Betty Jean advanced impatiently, while pouring water from a jug into the puppies' bowls.

"Sam I Am! Bad boy!" she called. "What are you doing to me today? Stop it." She grabbed him by the collar and backed him into a crate. Trainers and manuals warned never to approach a wary or fearful dog in this way. Never make direct eye contact, they insisted. Never advance straight on, never grab or tug. Betty Jean hadn't read these books. Her philosophy: Keep moving, show no fear.

She was a dervish, applying ointments to infected eyes, squirting disinfectants in crates and on floors, distributing worm medicine, checking on sutures from neutering procedures, pausing long enough to chat with a shy black Lab.

"Hey, sweet thing!" she cooed, breaking into a falsetto. "She's gonna be all right," she predicted. "I'm keeping her here because I don't like how shy she is around people. And I want to see her with kids. Nobody gets adopted until I'm sure. I won't have anybody getting bit. Of course you can't control how some *people* behave."

She turned to the playroom full of dogs and announced: "You all hear that? Nobody is getting adopted until I'm sure! So behave! And be quiet when I'm gone, or there'll be trouble. I do *not* want lots of noise here."

The one threat she wouldn't make, amid a stream of speeches about good citizenship, was: You're going back to the shelter. That has never happened. "No dog I take will ever go back to the shelter," she said. "End of discussion."

Suddenly, bedlam erupted as her own five dogs, a melange of sizes and breeds, broke out of her bedroom, where they stay apart from the rescued dogs. Betty Jean turned and clapped her hands: "Enough, all of you. No you don't, back into the bedroom. And I want quiet!" Like a circus act, her dogs thundered back into the bedroom.

Miraculously, given the number of ministrations, maneuvers, and mishaps, in an hour all the dogs were in their crates, which were draped with towels and curtains. Betty Jean turned down the lights and tuned the radio to a Spanish-language station.

"Oh, they love it," she explained. "Maybe because most of them come from the city. If you put rock or classical on, they'll bark all day. But the Latin music . . . they go right to sleep." Sure enough, two rooms that had been din and chaos five minutes earlier quieted down. Except for a whine or two from the puppies, instantly shushed by Betty Jean, and the percussive musical backup, the silence was almost eerie. From the outside, nobody could've told there was a dog in the house.

Betty Jean pulled her battered blue Ford Windstar—with 112,000 miles on the odometer, though it was barely four years old—alongside the other two vans. A clump of people were rearranging crates, boxes, and blankets. Puppies could be transported five or six to a crate, the bigger dogs singly in larger crates, the cats stuffed into cardboard boxes with holes. Denise, supervising the preparations, called hello.

Denise DiFurio was Betty Jean's energetic deputy and perhaps closest friend, though they spoke only of dogs and adoptions and never met or socialized in any other context. Denise worried about Betty Jean constantly—too little sleep, not enough food, no money or security, fragile health, no exercise, too much work, too much pressure. Her worries all seemed warranted, but Betty Jean brushed her fussing aside.

The record number of animals the group had ever taken from a shelter in a single day, Denise reported with some pride, was twenty-one: seven puppies, six adult dogs, plus cats and kittens. The attendant at the turnpike tollbooth nearly fainted at the smell, since several dogs had vomited or peed or defecated before they'd even made it out of Brooklyn. Rescued dogs are nervous and disoriented, often unhousebroken and unaccustomed to riding in cars.

So Save the Pets transporters drove "wide open"—windows down and vents blasting—even in bitter weather, the drivers bundled up in sweaters and hats.

The five commandos gathered to share mugs of coffee, pass around muffins, and go over plans for the mission. In particular, they talked about how many dogs they planned to take, although that number was always fluid, how many were going to Betty Jean, and how many were going elsewhere. They were all women, one married to a famously tolerant and much-praised husband, four divorced or never married. Apart from Denise, who served many functions, all basically transported dogs from New York, a steady source of abandoned animals, back to New Jersey. Occasionally, alerted by e-mail to a special case, they headed in other directions, too—to Bridgeport, Philadelphia, Newark, Trenton, as far as Boston.

None of the women introduced themselves. Dog rescue people, Betty Jean explained later, want attention focused on the animals, not themselves. "They just want homes for the dogs, that's the payoff," she said. "That great moment when you've got a dog and a person and they look at each other and they click, and you know they're gonna love each other and be okay. That really keeps us going. That's why we do it."

"Montclair is heaven for people like us," she added. "It's why I fight to live there, even though my kids are gone and the taxes are terrible. Lots of people with money, and they'll spend it on their dogs. They don't use them to guard gas stations. They want loved pets. We always perk up when we hear a Montclair person wants to adopt. That's what you want for any dog."

Then, as if reminding herself that this was enough slobbering sentimentality, she gave the order to move out.

There was some urgency to this Brooklyn trip. Betty Jean had gotten a call from her mole at the shelter that an unusually large number of dogs were about to be euthanized. The young woman in question had just given notice—she was moving on to college—and had phoned in this heads-up as a final gesture. Betty Jean and Denise lamented her departure, as it would force them to deal directly with the bureaucrats who ran the shelter, whom they mistrusted. Though they were ostensibly in the same business, shelters and rescue groups rarely got along.

Many shelter workers also join animal rescue

groups or work with rescue groups to save those animals in the shelters that are marked for execution or considered unadoptable. This insider had been a good friend to Save the Pets, tipping Betty Jean off to adoptable dogs that the shelter had given up on.

Their mole provided illicit access to the sickrooms and "death chambers" that the public never saw, reserved for the hard cases. When she wasn't on duty, the group had to pretend these rooms didn't exist, and that they hadn't been in them a thousand times, since they were officially off-limits to all but the shelter staff. Many shelters are wary: animal advocates often accuse them of killing dogs too quickly or cruelly, but the economics of dog sheltering are difficult; the longer a dog remains alive in a shelter, the more money it costs. The more space so-called unadoptable dogs take up, the less room for the adoptable ones.

The shelter directors wouldn't be pleased to know that members of Save the Pets were roaming the premises, let alone a writer. On the way to the Garden State Parkway, therefore, Betty Jean briefed me on the dangers and protocols of the trek. No notebooks, tape recorders, or cameras, she warned. I'd simply pass as a new volunteer. She wouldn't introduce me to their shelter friend. Nor would there be any questions or conversations.

As the vans approached the shelter, Betty Jean steeled herself, too, taking a deep breath. "The hard part is making choices," she said. "Denise or someone from the shelter might beg me to take a dog, but they're too soft-hearted. Denise would take every dog there if she could. We'd need an Amtrak train. So I decide. Somebody has to say no."

What she looked for, she said, was "a certain something in the dog's eyes—a connection, some affection. I know by now what people go for, what they will take. Otherwise . . ." She left the thought unfinished.

Betty Jean wasn't being imperious so much as protecting the other members of her group from what was clearly a searing process. Shelters got stuck with the worst by-products of America's tortured and complex relationship with dogs. Despite all the new work dogs are doing, millions face death every year. Rescue people hate to leave dogs behind to languish in crates or die. In a sense, dog rescue is about constant collisions with limits and reality. They want to save all the dogs, and their inability to do so is wrenching every time. It falls to Betty Jean to protect her group and to insist on some measure of reality, to keep the boundaries intact, to remind everyone that there are limits. There are things they can do, and there are things they can't.

Turning onto 280 East toward the Turnpike, we passed Newark Airport, belching refineries, acres of cargo containers. Betty Jean headed across Staten Island over the Verrazano Bridge and into deepest Brooklyn. It took more than an hour, even on a quiet Sunday morning.

The animal shelter was a low brick-and-concrete building on a busy street. Because it was barely eight A.M., there were empty parking spaces on the street. I went inside with Betty Jean and Denise; the others stayed outside with the vans.

Denise had brought along a digital camera. Some of the dogs would have to be left behind for microchipping—the shelter inserted an identifying chip beneath their skin so they can be identified if lost or abandoned—or shots or neutering. Others would go to vets for treatment before settling in at Betty Jean's or in temporary foster homes.

But their photographs would be posted on the Save the Pets website by nightfall; e-mail and calls about the cuter ones would begin to materialize in moments, as their digitized photos went whizzing around to other rescue groups and potential adopters.

Despite the millions of abandoned dogs, competition for the most adoptable (i.e., the most adorable) was so intense that sometimes other rescue groups tried to "rescue" dogs from groups like Save the Pets, so they'd have dogs available if people wanted them. By now, though, Denise, who along with her son served as webmaster, could spot such tactics.

The shelter smell hit us the minute the electronic doors opened—a combination of dogs, feces, disinfectant, and food. In the anteroom three immigrant families with halting English waited to see the dogs in the front room, ready for adoption. The kids were excited, straining for a look inside. Off to the side, a young man in a hooded sweatshirt, gold bracelets, and enormous sneakers stood next to a sobbing young woman. He was holding a pit bull, its body grotesquely twisted and bloodied; it was alive, but barely moving. The receptionist was asking him to fill out some forms. He was refusing.

"We've got to enter the dog into the system," the receptionist patiently explained.

"I got no time for this BS," the guy said sullenly. "I found the dog in the street, and because me and my girlfriend are so good-hearted, we had to pick it up and bring it over. I don't know anythin' about this dog, so you take it. That's what the cop said you was here for." And he placed the dog on the floor and turned to leave, over angry protests. The girl, still crying, leaned over to pat the dog goodbye, then followed her boyfriend toward the door.

Denise, perhaps noticing the girl's oddly intimate gesture, suddenly got into the young man's face. "This is your dog, isn't it? He was hit by a car and you don't want to pay the vet bills, so you just dumped him here, isn't that right?" Denise had a thick Brooklyn bray and an attitude: this was somebody who had no fear of a good, loud, attention-getting fight.

The guy glared, grabbed his girlfriend's hand, and pulled her along. "I told you we shoulda just dumped it outside," he snapped. The receptionist muttered something about calling the police. Denise looked pleadingly at Betty Jean.

"Put a hold on him," Betty Jean told the receptionist. "If he lives, we'll take him." She looked exasperated and turned away; Denise winked at me and smiled. An attendant came to slide the injured dog gently into a crate.

The mole appeared, greeted Betty Jean and Denise by name, and hugged them. Betty Jean had talked on the drive over about how hard shelter work was for the dog lovers on the staff, who soon discovered that human beings are capable of dreadful things, and that even the best shelters can turn into slaughterhouses because so many dogs pour into the system. Many staffers are young women who want to help animals, and the job isn't what they expect. It wears them out. Rescue is easier in one way, Betty Jean said. You don't have to watch dogs die all day.

The four of us moved briskly through the waiting room, down a series of corridors, past clean rooms filled with stainless-steel crates. The dogs weren't visible from the hall, but the rooms were labeled: SICK, SURGERY, and CAUTION.

The main display room near the entrance held a score of dogs who looked healthy and relatively attractive, some quite appealing. But farther back, things got uglier. Some dogs had sores, or missing limbs, or had clearly been beaten. (Two had been found alive in garbage bags near Coney Island,

71

multiple bones broken.) Betty Jean's friend rattled off a litany of sad histories: a Lab found starving near its owner's dead body; a retriever whose owners moved away, leaving him wandering in the street; a poodle who'd survived a car crash but whose people hadn't; a border collie mix who had been used as bait to train fighting pit bulls; a shell-shocked puppy who'd been doused with gasoline and set afire.

One room held a variety of ferocious fighting dogs seized by the police or abandoned once they'd been bested in a match—barrel-chested pit bulls, mixed breeds, imports from Africa and Asia, a scarred mastiff. They roared when the doors opened and threw themselves at their crates. Not long for this world, said Betty Jean.

We were being escorted to a room for adoptable dogs and cats with minor ailments—worms, skin infections, lesions. If the shelter could heal them and put them out front, it could charge a $100 adoption fee. The rescue people paid only a token fee if the dogs were especially sick, $40 plus various small fees if they were healthy. Betty Jean suspected that the shelter hid some of the more appealing dogs from rescuers in the hope that they could restore their health and then charge the higher price.

Beyond the money the adoptions generated, municipal shelters liked having appealing dogs to adopt—it justified their existence and was good public relations. Nothing pulls at the heartstrings more than a sweet dog awaiting a family. Nothing leaves most hearts colder than a beat-up pit bull.

Betty Jean was, as promised, decisive, almost ruthless. She gave the nod to several, including a ratty, battered-looking miniature poodle. "We'll take her," she said. "People love lap dogs; we can always place them."

Denise came dashing over like an excited kid. "Betty Jean, there's a dog back there we have to have—" Betty Jean held up her hand.

"Is it a pit? *Is* it?"

Denise started to mumble, then said yes.

"No more pits!" Betty Jean was emphatic. "I can't place them in Montclair, and it's expensive to feed them. People don't want them, right or wrong. We can't afford to take dogs people don't want."

Denise was a sucker for hard-to-place dogs, but she acknowledged Betty Jean's point: always financially strapped, Save the Pets really couldn't house unwanted dogs for years. She didn't push.

Suddenly, the two women froze outside a large crate. It held a ten-year-old yellow Lab with heart problems whose elderly owners had been seriously injured in an auto accident. The dog had been brought in by the couple's daughter, who was, she regretted, allergic to dogs.

Betty Jean teared up. The dog, its glazed eyes still open, had died. It hadn't eaten since coming in two weeks earlier, their shelter ally reported soberly. "She gave up," she said. "You could see it. She couldn't take it here."

Betty Jean tightened her lips. "We could have placed that dog in a second. It didn't have to die here alone." Some older dogs just can't take the separation, the confinement, the din. The mole left to find somebody to remove the body. She brought back word that the pit left in the lobby when they'd first come in was dead, too.

She pulled Betty Jean over into a corner and whispered to her. Betty Jean was getting fidgety—it was dangerous to linger too long at the shelter, she felt. Officials might spot them in places where they shouldn't be, which could get their mole in trouble. It was exhausting, and she never liked to leave the dogs back in Jersey alone for more than a few hours. But she nodded and the odd group wound its way back through a mazelike series of hallways to a small room, housing some pits, rotties, and mixed-breed strays, all scheduled for euthanasia the coming week. The aide pointed to a crate stacked up high, holding a small black Lab-like puppy lying on its side, bandages wrapped around its shoulders and neck, its eyes encrusted with dried mucus. The prognosis wasn't good, the shelter worker told Betty Jean, and even to an untrained eye, the puppy looked in dreadful shape. The crate's label said the dog was female, about twelve weeks old, suffering from infected dog bites and wounds, malnutrition, dehydration, and severe conjunctivitis. It might be blind. The puppy had been left outside a rowhouse, tied to a telephone pole, the aide reported with disgust.

74

Neighborhood dogs had attacked it; a sanitation worker had brought it to the shelter.

"Hey there," Betty Jean murmured. The dog didn't respond. Apart from its chest moving slowly, it could have been dead already.

"If you can," the mole murmured, "do it for me. There's something about this dog. She's too young. She probably won't make it, but she has no chance in here. Maybe . . ."

Betty Jean didn't need to hear more. "I'll take her home. Let's call her Hopeless."

Since the dog had been labeled unsuitable for adoption, there would be no paperwork. The mole would simply wrap Hopeless in a blanket and carry her out the back door to Betty Jean's van. "Hell, I've got nothing to lose. I'm out of here anyway," she said.

"It might be too late," Betty Jean cautioned, businesslike again. "I can't do miracles."

The mole suddenly enveloped her in a hug. They would probably never see each other again, after three years of conspiring.

"We did some good," said the worker.

Always careful about showing too much emotion, Betty Jean patted her young ally's back and said nothing. She didn't really have to. Besides, she didn't have time for emotion; it would eat her up.

Fifteen minutes later, Betty Jean and Denise were filling out forms for eighteen dogs, twelve already microchipped and ready to leave, plus eight

75

cats, all set to go; the others would be picked up in two days.

The other Save the Pets members came in to tote out the cats in cardboard boxes and put the dogs on leashes; they'd be crated and placed carefully in vans. They'd all go to various vets over the next few days—some for neutering, others to be examined and immunized—before any could go into foster homes.

A half hour later, the animals were loaded, cats yowling, a couple of dogs barking and clawing at the crates, puppies whining, the rescuers physically and emotionally spent.

Betty Jean looked pale; even the garrulous Denise was uncharacteristically tense. "We all hate coming here even though it's what we do," Denise said. "You want to take them all home, but you just can't."

Betty Jean nodded. "You can't help but think of the ones you leave behind. That's what nobody understands. You're sentencing dogs to death, even while you're rescuing them. You just have to do what you can . . ."

"And you do a lot more than that," Denise interjected.

Betty Jean, cradling the swathed Hopeless in one arm, checked the configuration of crates, filled water bowls, sprinkled kibble around, tried to reassure the terrified cats. She was taking home three puppies and three dogs herself.

But first, a stop at the White Castle across the

street. At the drive-through, Betty Jean would order a large Coke and half a dozen hamburgers; she was starving. "I haven't had a regular meal in a few days," she said self-consciously. "I eat in bunches."

Denise couldn't help chiming in. "She never eats. She's always feeding the dogs, but she herself never eats."

Betty Jean looked mildly embarrassed. "I don't have time to cook meals," she said. "I don't even have time to eat them."

Pulling over outside the White Castle, she wolfed down one burger after another, washed down with gulps of soda. Then she announced that she could eat a little more and turned back through the drive-through for another giant Coke, six more burgers, plus an order of fries. The fast-food smell added yet another note to the already powerful range of odors in the van. She and the other drivers steamed their way back to Jersey, carrying their odd cargo, plucked from the mean streets and headed for the L.L. Bean cedar beds, play groups, and gourmet treats that mark animal life in Montclair.

What does it say about a country that's developed an extraordinarily sophisticated and comprehensive structure for saving dogs, but no equivalent one for rescuing endangered or troubled people? Few human-animal interactions spawn as many moral questions as the dog rescue movement.

Why are there so many millions of dogs in need

of rescuing, and so many people eager to do rescues and adopt the rescuees? Is this the underside of the new work of dogs, the animal casualties of emotional irresponsibility, of unrealistic expectations? Or are these dogs the by-products of a culture that mass-markets the *idea* of dogs but takes no responsibility for the excess production or the inevitable problems it causes?

One might argue that we're not doing anything to dogs we're not doing to the elderly, the mentally ill, and homeless, perhaps even to the spouses, companions, and partners we leave in substantial numbers. Dogs are simply another symptom of a general inability to commit.

But the treatment of dogs is different from the treatment of humans. The elderly, disabled, and homeless are presumed to have rights; a wealth of laws and court cases regulate their treatment and welfare. Dogs have less protection. And humans, theoretically at least, can give voice to their grievances and desires. Dogs can't communicate effectively and can be easily removed by driving to an animal shelter or calling a rescue group.

Lots of solutions to the unwanted-animal issue have been proposed, but in an era of scarce civic resources, when allocation of public money is so fiercely debated, local governments are unlikely to spend more on animal-control projects like neutering, licensing, providing veterinary care, or constructing additional, more humane, shelters.

Few other species require so much salvaging,

and get so much. Yet despite all that effort and the explosive growth of the rescue movement, up to 5 million unwanted dogs are still killed each year.

Save the Pet's arduous treks into Brooklyn barely make a dent. In 2001, some 50,600 dogs and cats entered New York City's animal welfare system, according to *The New York Times*. Of those, 36,500 (or 72 percent) were killed, an average of a hundred a day. Small wonder Betty Jean grew depressed afterward.

"Denise is always telling me I do too much. But I know I do too little. Look what I leave behind."

No outsider can know how accurately the rescuers are assessing these shelter dogs. Invariably angry, often bordering on the paranoid, the rescuers are convinced that shelters hide dogs from them so that they can charge higher fees; that sick dogs are condemned without sufficient medical care; that aggressive or abused dogs that could be retrained and reclaimed are given up on. They're convinced they run a perpetual and losing race to save worthy, adoptable dogs from the executioner's needle.

Shelters point out in reply that they have little money, too little staff, and inadequate facilities, that they are low on the list of taxpayers' priorities. So they are overwhelmed by the volume of abandoned, often ill, sometimes aggressive dogs. On top of that, they're beset by animal advocates who want "no-kill" policies at every shelter and by rescuers whom they can never hope to please.

"These rescue groups do wonderful work and save so many dogs and they bring lots of love into people's homes," says a Montclair shelter official. "But the truth is that they sometimes value dogs over people and would like a world in which no dog is ever put down, no matter how unadoptable, aggressive, or unwanted. But we can't keep all these dogs alive. There is no space or food or money. We have to make choices. Besides," she added, "if people have to vote whether to support schools or keep dogs and cats alive, well, maybe education is more important than dog pounds."

Many rescue workers do, in fact, sound perpetually suspicious of politicians, contemptuous of what seems an uncaring public, even resentful of the care lavished on children in towns like Montclair. Some joke that they'd rather make room in parks for dogs than for more "brats." They, on the other hand, are doing crucial work. At least they believe they're making a difference—the very things so many Americans find it difficult to feel.

It took Betty Jean half an hour to get the new arrivals settled, a messy task. She put Hopeless in a basket on the kitchen table so she could keep one eye on her, then whizzed back and forth, repeating the morning routine, but much more tired now.

Hopeless, on closer examination, looked to be a beauty, the kind that would have flown out of the shelter if she were in good health. But, then, Betty

Jean said, she probably wouldn't have been there if she'd been healthy.

"Maybe we should've called her 'Hopeful,'" she mused. But she didn't change the name. Like so many other aspects of rescue, this was her call to make.

She trusted only herself to decide which dogs should be rescued, and when they were ready for adoption. She relied on no one else to make sure her dogs were fed, walked, trained. She alone determined which adoptions should proceed, which shouldn't.

And she could be quite peremptory about that. One evening the doorbell rang, setting off the now-predictable clamor; a middle-aged couple from Boonton were coming to look at Bugs, a Lab-shepherd mix two weeks out of the Brooklyn shelter. Bugs was shy and wary when he first arrived, but now bounded out of his crate and into the yard with enthusiasm. Betty Jean, who had a soft spot for him, was training him to sit.

The Boonton woman, who'd been calling and e-mailing Betty Jean for months, said she had been lobbying her husband for a dog and had recently spotted Bugs on the Save the Pets website. The husband had balked at first, but she'd been pleading for so long that his resistance was wearing down.

Alice and Bugs, named for his big eyes, seemed to click right away. He rolled in her lap, licked her hand. Harvey and Bugs didn't click; the dog ignored his calls and moved away from his outstretched palm.

And then there was Harvey's first question: "How much? It says on your website that adoptions are free, but then when you read the small print . . ."

Betty Jean stiffened but explained. "It costs a lot to take care of a dog like Bugs." Normally, she asked for a $70 donation. "We have to pay the shelter, transport and feed the dog, take him to the vet for neutering and shots. But we don't charge if everything else works out and you can't afford to pay."

Harvey waved his hand dismissively, as if to say he was used to this sort of run-around. "Come here, boy," he said, a bit gruffly. Bugs moved closer, somewhat reluctantly, then edged back toward Alice. Harvey said he'd like to think about it, discuss the matter with his wife.

"Sorry you came all this way," Betty Jean announced in her authoritative tone. "But you can't take him."

Alice looked incredulous; Harvey insisted on an explanation. He got one.

"One, I don't give dogs to people whose opening question is 'How much?' That's never the first thing people ask when they love a dog, because dogs cost a lot of money," Betty Jean told him. "If you're worried about our fee, then how are you going to feel when you're taking him to the vet for two hundred dollars' worth of shots?" Harvey stood

82

up, his face turning ruddy. Bugs backed toward Betty Jean.

"Two, it's really your wife who wants a dog. That's trouble, too. It's got to be a family decision, and you aren't really interested.

"And finally, I'm sure you're a nice man," Betty Jean said, although with no particular conviction, "but I just don't feel right about this adoption, and I have to feel right. I didn't bring this dog all this way for him to be unhappy or wind up in another shelter. So"—she went to open the door for Alice and Harvey—"why don't you think about this whole thing some more?" And that was that.

"No way that guy is getting a dog from me," she muttered as she closed the door behind them. She went over to her computer and typed his name into a database for future reference, along with the woman from Upper Montclair who'd called to ask if Betty Jean had any dog that might go with her new russet sofa.

Somebody else might have taken a flier on this couple, or assigned a checker to monitor the home and make sure things were going well. Betty Jean had a lot of dogs to place, and more were coming from Brooklyn in a few days; she could have used the emptied crate. But she couldn't turn off her bedrock feelings about trust, responsibility, and an empathic obsession to see that Bugs never felt unwanted or unsafe again.

Another evening revealed a bit more about why she might feel that way.

Betty Jean doesn't like to get very personal—"None of this is about me, it's about the dogs"—but she reluctantly confirmed a few bare-bones details about her past. She grew up in the 1940s in Germany, where her parents and siblings were all killed—she would not say how. She moved from one bombed-out village to another before a relative living in the United States sent her a plane ticket. She professed little memory of her early childhood and no wish to probe much further. "I remember it was hard, but why dig it all back up again? My regular life has been tough enough."

In America, she married an ironworker and had three children, two sons and a daughter. They were perpetually broke and she and her husband quarreled ceaselessly before he left in 1984, two years after she'd begun one of New Jersey's earliest rescue groups. Betty Jean had a visceral disgust for whining and complaining, and little patience for the distinctly American culture of self-revelatory victimization. Her marriage was bad, she said, but that was life. Other people had it worse.

She rarely sees her children or four grandchildren these days, although they live fairly nearby. Her daughter calls every week—"She's stubborn, like me"—and asks her to spend some time with her two small children. Betty Jean tells her the same thing each time: She's terribly busy and doesn't have time.

"I've done that, and it's somebody else's turn," she said with a shrug. "The dogs need my time and attention. They can't be left for long." Her sons, hurt and angry, gave up long ago and now call only rarely.

She wasn't very forthcoming about this struggle. "I do what I have to do" was her mantra. Yet she kept framed photos of her kids and grandkids around the living room—lots of them.

Almost irrationally generous with her money and time when it came to her group and the animals it rescued, she could sound petty when talking about her family, who were dubious about her deepening involvement in dog rescue.

"They just want a baby-sitter. I'm not a baby-sitter," she'd say defensively. Or, "I can't afford to be calling grandchildren all the time. I have to save my money for calls about adoption, for time online posting pictures of the dogs and answering all my e-mail."

And then: "You see, I just don't have time. I don't have time to eat. I don't have time to shop. I hardly get to see my own dogs. That's the way it is."

That part seemed true: the life she had built didn't have a spare second in it.

Take Hopeless, for example, whose eyes were finally clearing up under Betty Jean's continuing ministrations. She kept the puppy with her all day, smuggling her into the office in a canvas tote, so she could administer the medications a sympathetic vet had given her gratis. But otherwise, the dog still barely moved or ate, nor did it respond to the vitamins and other medications Betty Jean was literally forcing down her throat. She was draped inertly across her lap now, as Betty Jean massaged her back.

A happier story was Danny, a mammoth black Labrador she'd found at the Brooklyn shelter and kept for herself. "My soulmate," she called him. When she let him out of the bedroom that evening, they exchanged kisses and hugs for a minute or two, until she ordered him back inside so she could take care of the other dogs and answer her e-mail.

"My favorite time of day," she said, allowing a rare smile, "is the few minutes every evening before bedtime. My dogs and I all cuddle up in bed together, and I tell them about my day, and they tell me about theirs. I love that. But I usually fall asleep with the lights still on."

Betty Jean did make a few concessions to family life. She took a brief break for an annual family trek to the Jersey shore—a single summer afternoon—and she had Christmas dinner at her daughter's house. They were not pleasant occasions, it appears, in part because her family worried about the depth of her involvement with dog rescue, and because she was constantly distracted, worrying about some problem back home. "What if a water pipe burst? What if a fire broke out? What would happen to the dogs?" she demanded angrily, as if the dangers of leaving them for family events should be as evident to everyone else as it was to her. On the other hand, she couldn't host the gathering herself—her house wasn't a good place for small children—and there was little to suggest she wanted to.

She looked almost longingly at the framed picture of her grandsons on a living room table. "I wouldn't have any place for them even to sit. And I'd have to watch them every second. What if something happened to them? What if they got bit?" She almost winced when she talked about her children.

It wasn't always this way. "We had some fun here in this house," she said. "Trips, friends, but that was quite a long time ago." She grew dreamy when she talked about those days, memories from another world, so different from her current routine.

She roused herself. "They know me. They know I will do what I have to do," she said, shutting off even these sparse details. "I've always had to work in office jobs that I hate with nasty bosses, but my real life, my real work, is the dogs."

After considerable urging, she thought back to the day two decades earlier when it all began. She hadn't even owned a dog before then. But a small ugly brown mutt, a stray, showed up at her door one day looking hungry, so she gave him some leftover hamburger. She brought him to PAWS, the local animal shelter—her first trip to a shelter—but she was shocked by what she saw and couldn't bring herself to leave him there. She began volunteering one afternoon a week, and then, over time, two or three days. "I knew this was the work I was meant to do," she recalls.

Rescue people all tell variations of the same story. They came across this dog. They took it in. They began volunteering. Soon, they were bringing dogs home and looking for other people to take them in.

"I had no idea, no idea," Betty Jean said. "Maybe I should have left him outside."

Which suggests that she knew the rescuing had taken her over, and that she found that acceptable. Other Save the Pets members had to take her car in for service; otherwise she forgot, as she forgot to get her license and registration renewed on time. Her phone service got cut off periodically, when there wasn't enough money in her account for automatic payment and she forgot to send a check. She did manage to keep her homeowners' insurance in force. God only knows what would happen if the insurance company discovered how many stray dogs from Brooklyn were filling her house.

Because of all the dogs, the house was never empty long enough to have work done on it, so the paint Betty Jean looked at was the paint she saw when she moved in almost four decades ago. She hadn't been to a movie in years. She rarely even watched TV, since she was taking care of dogs nonstop till eight-thirty or later and invariably passed out by nine.

The only vacation she'd allowed herself since the early 1970s was a trip with Denise out to visit the

Best Friends Animal Sanctuary in Knabb, Utah. The leader of a rescue group had bought an enormous property there and sheltered at least 1,800 dogs and cats from all over the country, some to be put up for adoption, many to live out their lives. It was, she assured me, the best vacation of her life.

She was especially drawn to the sanctuary's subdivision called Dogtown, which had its own Town Hall and adoption center. Dogtown's website (at www.bestfriends.org) directed its messages to the dogs themselves:

"Within a few days, you're getting the hang of it. You're in a group of maybe five or six dogs and you're making friends, playing games, big breakfast in the morning, and treats in the afternoon. Nice walks, too, and lots of afternoon snoozes and your own special person to look after you. And tons of visitors who love hugs and kisses and want their photos taken with you and just can't get enough of it when you and your pals show off to them.

"Maybe," the site concludes, "the world isn't such a bad place after all!"

Betty Jean smiled. "None of them ever gets put down. I'd love to do that."

Dogtown's description was perhaps more revealing than its authors intended. It went to the heart of the dog rescue ethos: Maybe we can't build a perfect world for ourselves, but we can try like hell to create a perfect world for you.

Soon after this conversation, a member of Save

the Pets told me that a relative of Betty Jean's had shown up at an adoption fair one day, and that Betty Jean was so unnerved by his appearance that she had to go inside her van and sit there.

Betty Jean had told her a bit, just a few words, about the night her family was blown to bits by Allied bombs while everyone sat at the dinner table. She'd watched her entire existence disintegrate. Her remaining relatives had all lost contact with her after she married, and she never replied to calls or letters.

But when I asked about this story, Betty Jean shrugged, her eyes vacant. She had nothing more to say about her past, she said. She had too many things to worry about in the present.

Two days before Thanksgiving, the dozen active members of Save the Pets gathered for lunch, the only time all year that they were all assembled together, in the flesh, rather than communicating by e-mail or phone, or sprinting into the city in twos or threes or to one another's homes to move dogs around.

They convened at one of those suburban steakhouses in a neighboring town, the prefab menu and ersatz old-timey decor rendering each restaurant indistinguishable from the others in the chain. Save the Pets, Inc., met at this restaurant every year—it was centrally located—and gathered around one long table.

The lunch was part holiday get-together but

mostly a gesture of appreciation for Betty Jean. Denise joked it was a way of making sure Betty Jean got at least one good meal per year. Everyone at the table had brought a gift or card for her. They'd also all heard rumors about her health. She looked exhausted and was suffering from severe stomach cramps. In fact, she barely touched her food.

The lunch was unstructured, informal, a little hurried. Almost everybody had day jobs or classes to get back to, and few of them really knew each other all that well. They weren't terribly social people anyway. But the conversation flowed, as long as it was about dogs.

At one end of the table, two women were trading horror stories about the city shelters. In the middle, the talk drifted toward difficult dogs—biters, jumpers, chewers, runners—that had been fostered and happily turned around, or "flipped."

They all had specific roles in the organization. Denise and Andy and Patricia, the group's three transporters, spent hours driving to shelters, battling with the bureaucrats there, ferrying the rescued dogs to vets and then to foster homes.

Dr. Jannissey, the vet who worked with the group, stopped by, and the "checkers"—three had shown up—gave him a rousing cheer. They vetted people and homes to make sure they were legit and appropriate, paying as much attention to the people as to the dogs. Was the prospective owner too preoccupied with looks or color? Did the whole family want the dog, or just a lonely spouse or kid? Did anybody in the household appear gruff or short-tempered? Was somebody home much of the day? What about the yard? Nearby parks? Was there enough money to support a dog? Enough patience?

One checker—Pat, from Verona—told Jannissey she had pulled a dog out of a house just a week earlier, after she learned that the couple had lied about their jobs: they didn't work at home but were gone all day, sometimes well into the evening. Pat sat outside until they got home, at nearly nine P. M., and marched the dog right out of the house under their astonished noses.

Like most towns, Montclair limits the number of dogs in a home (to four), but "fosterers" like Audrey and her fourteen-year-old daughter Maggie had housed as many as fifteen, although usually many fewer. The township wasn't actually interested in forcing its way into houses and counting dogs, so there was usually no trouble unless the neighbors complained.

"This is great for her," Audrey said of her shy, silent daughter, seated next to her. "She was hanging around the house a lot. She didn't have a lot of friends. She loves this work . . ." Maggie nodded. When I asked her questions, her mother answered for her.

Though the fosterers didn't dash around as much as the rescuers, their jobs were also emotionally draining. Their charges were sometimes sick or abused, sometimes aggressive, usually untrained and unsocialized. The fosterers took them in, named them, loved them, exercised and observed and evaluated them, played with them, exposed them to a variety of real-world situations. Their mission was to ready the dogs for adoption, and seeing some of the dogs they fostered, it was hard to believe that would ever happen. In fact, however, though it sometimes took years, their adoption rate was 95 percent.

Only a dog who was irretrievably ill or truly dangerous was put down. It has happened just three or four times in the years Save the Pets has been operating.

The constant flow of animals represented almost the opposite of the typical dog experience, which is about attachment. Remember Angel, who chewed through a wall and a sofa and then, for good measure, gnawed off much of a spare tire?—the fosterers reminisced. And Scooter, who jumped through a screen door and ate a chunk of mailbag before they could stop him? And who tried to bite Audrey a hundred times before she finally won his trust? (Audrey was still dealing with the Postal Service on the mail incident.) And then, suddenly, young Maggie was crying and everyone else was comforting her down at her end of the table. Betty Jean, who missed nothing, asked what was wrong.

Audrey knew right away. They'd spent two years socializing a mean mutt named Pullman, who'd bitten a half-dozen people, including Audrey and her then-husband. Even Betty Jean was about to give up on him, but Maggie spent hours with the dog every day, feeding and stroking him, walking and exercising him, reading him stories and talking to him from outside his crate.

Everybody at the table remembered him, none fondly, but Maggie had stayed with Pullman, reassuring and training him, winning his trust.

An unwritten rule of fostering is that any relationship with a rescue dog is temporary. The volunteer is only a way station on this strange canine underground railroad, not an owner, not a home. So on the appointed day, Audrey and Maggie bathed the reformed Pullman so that he'd be presentable at one of Betty Jean's adoption fairs. Then Audrey's ex came in and left the door unlatched. Pullman was out of the house in a flash, and died instantly under the wheels of a New Jersey Transit bus.

Betty Jean, reminded of Maggie's loss, came over and touched her shoulder. "But remember how many dogs you've saved, how many are alive and happy," she said. For a few minutes, Maggie seemed inconsolable. Audrey leaned over, whispering in her ear, rubbing her back.

Then Maggie recovered a bit and the lunch went on.

All during the lunch, such stories, some equally horrific, bounced back and forth, the members of the group jawing like old ballplayers recounting their big games and breathtaking plays.

This was familiar ground. Maggie was a kid, so she took it harder, but the random, often cruel nature of dogs' lives and deaths was something everybody at the lunch knew a lot about. "We are," said Audrey, "the paramedics of the dog world. We see everything."

Betty Jean, who'd brought a few inexpensive gifts, gave Maggie her present early—a bottle of cologne with the CVS sticker still stuck on the bottom. Standard protocol: the group knew that Betty Jean had no money. They exclaimed politely over the trinkets she distributed, but the more important gifts were the ones they'd pooled their contributions to buy for her.

This year, the members of Save the Pets gave its founder a gift certificate to White Castle for one hundred burgers, a marker redeemable for three dog crates from a local pet store, a thousand dollars' worth of free medical care from a local group veterinary practice (that gift would keep on giving for about three weeks, chuckled Betty Jean), a case of Lysol, three boxes of paper towels, and two forty-pound bags of puppy food, which excited Betty Jean more than anything.

"Now *this* is something," she exclaimed. "I have so much need for puppy food!"

It was impossible not to be struck by the way the others loved her, respected her, worriedly monitored her, praised the way she had virtually turned over her life to rescuing and placing the dregs, castaways, and lost souls of the dog world. She was the center, the glue.

After the gift-giving, Denise clinked her spoon against the water glass. Dressed in a festive red and green sweater and pants with a plastic wreath around her neck, she acted as the awkward emcee. The group wasn't into speech-making, and Betty Jean would get uncomfortable if too much attention was drawn to her.

"I don't want to talk long, because I know most of you are busy. But I just want to say Happy Thanksgiving and Merry Christmas. And thank you. And a special thanks for Betty Jean, who does so much great work, has such a great heart, and who is the soul of Save the Pets. She's a saint. A saint. God bless her!" The group toasted. Betty Jean looked uncomfortable but nodded. She was, Denise confided, much too shy to say anything herself. But she circled the table twice to thank everybody personally for all the work they had done.

And to tell the truth, given how much effort it took to rescue a single dog, the group's scorecard was impressive. In the past year Save the Pets, Inc., had rescued more than five hundred dogs and placed almost all of them in homes.

Saturdays were adoption days. While most Montclair residents were pushing their kids in strollers, preparing brunch, or poring over *The New York Times*, Betty Jean got up even earlier than usual on a bright morning before Christmas. This was one of Save the Pet's prime adoption periods: so many parents would love nothing more than to present their kids with a puppy on Christmas morning. So Betty Jean's split-level was bursting with dogs.

This Saturday she would set up shop outside a pet store. Next week she'd hit the high school's annual holiday musical extravaganza. This wasn't strictly legal; she didn't have a permit or permission, but everybody looked the other way, especially at Christmastime. The faithful Denise, along with Audrey and Maggie, had promised to help out at several locations.

"It's our busiest time," Betty Jean said. "We have to make the most of it."

Adoption days were even more frantic than shelter-visit days. She had to not only feed, medicate, water, and exercise all the dogs, but decide which ones to stuff into her van for adoption.

This presented the usual dilemma. She could bring the hard cases—the pit bulls and rottie mixes people were often leery of—or the easy ones, the poodles, Lab mixes, and puppies most likely to be adopted. Too many of the latter meant the tougher dogs would languish longer without homes. Too many of the tough dogs, though, and people might come to associate Save the Pets with undesirable and unadoptable dogs.

One crate was already in the car, covered by a quilt. Betty Jean shot me an uncharacteristically coy look. "A surprise," she said.

Then she clicked into manic overdrive, racing back and forth with food, water, ointments, and medications, opening crates, letting dogs out and in, cooing, warming, shushing. Adoption days were difficult; she might be relinquishing dogs she had brought back, almost literally, from the abyss.

"It's tough saying goodbye all the time," she conceded. "Usually I can't do it, I can't look at them. Let's face it, we've been through a lot together."

But by eight-forty-five the van was loaded: three cats in cardboard boxes with air holes, seven dogs in four crates jammed ingeniously into the car.

She went into the garage and hauled out a fading wooden sandwich sign that announced: "Pet Adoption Today." She filled a jug with water, put some kibble in a plastic pouch, grabbed bowls, doggie bags, and toys. People loved to see the dogs playing, she said.

On the way to the pet store, she practiced her pitch for each dog. Sammy is a Lab mix, she'd say, who is sweet around women but needs some work around men. Ham is a rottweiler puppy who loves people and other dogs. Stormy, aptly named, needs a lot of room to run and somebody who can spend time with him throughout the day. Pickles, a collie-mutt mix, is a good apartment dog, older and not especially energetic. (Betty Jean conceded that when in doubt about a dog's lineage, she threw "Lab" or "retriever" in there somehow; people tended to see those breeds as friendly and

98

adoptable.) She didn't make up cat stories; people who wanted cats didn't seem to need them.

She pulled into the pet-store parking lot, accompanied by whining and meowing from the rear of the van, and before unloading went inside to greet the store owner, a supporter who always sent her off with bags of food, slightly damaged or returned toys, shampoos, and jugs of odor-killers.

Next, Denise arrived, followed shortly by Audrey and Maggie bringing an older golden retriever who'd recently graduated from foster care. Maggie gently guided him out of the crate and sat down next to him on the sidewalk. He licked her hand, wagged his tail. He had been bathed and groomed for the occasion. The very first people who came by, a couple in their sixties, fell in love with him, and went off to be grilled by Denise and Audrey.

Nobody took home a Save the Pets dog without a long conversation about his or her personal life, habits, moods, living arrangements, and sense of responsibility. Anybody who bristled at intrusive personal questions—and many did—was politely told to go somewhere else for a dog. "What's the big deal? It's only a dog" was a conversation-ender.

This couple didn't pass; their apartment was tiny, they had no yard, and both were in frail health. Betty Jean vetoed the adoption: If one of them got sick, who would take care of the dog? The dog had already been through enough.

Even when Betty Jean agreed, the adoption process took several days, during which a "screener" visited the prospective home and asked lots more questions. It was all carefully designed to give adopters plenty of time to think things over and be sure.

Betty Jean decided a woman interested in one of the puppies wasn't right—not at home enough. The rott puppy, though, went to a young couple from Vernon who'd seen his photo on the website. They had five acres in rural Sussex County. Sold.

An enormous woman in tight spandex pants and with big Jersey hair, a shopper not even thinking of dogs, shrieked with joy when she spotted Charlie, an obese, drooling, elderly bulldog who had already attended a dozen adoption fairs without success. In a minute, the two were embracing on the sidewalk, madly in love. Sometimes, said Betty Jean, things just click.

"Okay," Betty Jean announced shortly before ten A.M. "Now, the surprise." She pulled out the covered crate, lifted off the quilt, and beamed.

"Hopeless!" she declared theatrically, as if for an entire audience waiting in breathless suspense. If she hadn't said the name, the pup would have been unrecognizable. Her eyes were clear, the bandages gone; she was as lively, animated, and friendly as Lab puppies were supposed to be, her tail flailing at every living thing that passed by, two legs or four. When Betty Jean opened the crate, Hopeless jumped into her arms, climbed up her chest, slobbered all over her face. Apart from a few scars where she had been mauled, Hopeless looked great, an adorable dog. And a staggering amount of work. Just how much, or under what circumstances, hardly anyone would ever know.

As if locked on by radar, a family of four—the Schusters, Hank, Gloria, and their seven-year-old twins—descended on Betty Jean and the dog.

It seemed a match from the start. Hank, a Wall Street type, worked in the city, while Gloria, a schoolteacher by trade, was at home full-time now, taking care of the kids. There were no other animals in the house. They had a spacious yard and would agree, in writing, to fence most of it for Hopeless to romp in.

They understood that the dog must be spayed after they adopted it, and that if they failed to do so, Save the Pets checkers might repossess her. They readily agreed to the seventy-dollar fee and offered to throw in another hundred as a donation. Without prompting, both parents mentioned the need for professional training to make sure the puppy—which they understood would grow up to be a large and powerful dog—knew how to behave.

This was crucial to Betty Jean; it was the untrained dogs who were most likely to bounce back. She also probed to be sure the parents didn't really believe the two kids would be totally responsible for dog care; she knew they'd be back to watching TV and playing computer games within days.

Nobody looked standoffish, inflexible, or squeamish. In fact, every member of the family was down on the ground, patting and hugging the dog. And Hopeless was in a happy frenzy, licking, chewing, squirming. This was probably more attention than she had received in her entire short but unhappy life—except for the six weeks in Betty Jean's care. Another testament to the sometimes amazing adaptability of dogs, given the right circumstances.

"Let's get the paperwork started," she said. "I think this could work out."

After a few minutes, the twins were saying dramatic farewells to Hopeless, who was going back into her crate and the van until the screeners had checked out the home. Meanwhile, there were other dogs to spotlight.

Hank Schuster had a question about the preliminary adoption forms and turned to look for Betty Jean. But she wasn't there. She'd gone into the van, for "just a second," she said, and was sitting behind the steering wheel, dabbing at her eyes with a tissue.

CHAPTER 4

MORE THAN A FRIEND

At 4:40 A.M. every day of the week—rain, shine, or snow—the digital alarm beeped softly. Rob Cochran got up, tested his bum knee with the full weight of his 230-pound frame, and winced; it always hurt when he first put pressure on it. He tiptoed into the bathroom so as not to wake his wife, Judy, or the three kids sleeping down the long hallway, then drowsily stepped into his walking shoes, a battered old pair of jeans and a polo shirt, a sweatshirt or parka depending on weather and season.

He went downstairs to the laundry room and opened the door for a dog so big, black, and unruly that he might be mistaken for a bear.

Cherokee, happy to see Rob, banged into door and walls, excited, panting, then rushing over to his food bowl in the kitchen. If there wasn't something in it, and soon, the barking could wake the dead, not to mention the family. The coffeemaker was already gurgling. Rob had set it the night before; he wouldn't have time to fuss with coffee when he returned from his walk.

He needed to be back by 6:30 at the latest in order to shower, change, collect his papers, and then half-trot the five blocks to the DeCamp bus into Manhattan, where he was a senior partner at a busy and successful, if not absolutely top-tier, firm specializing in corporate criminal law.

The last few years had been good to Rob—good enough to spend more than $600,000 for this gracious, six-bedroom, four-bath Tudor. But like most successes, his came at a cost: long and arduous days, lots of stress, a cell phone that was never out of reach, "homework" almost every night.

He worked on the commute into Manhattan and on the way out, too. "We're so dumb we've added three hours to the workday," he lamented, "and nobody gets paid for it."

Despite the pressure, he was a confident, successful, self-assured, imposing man, in pretty good shape at forty-eight, even with that knee, if unable to entirely fend off a bit of the paunch that characterized so many of his friends and neighbors. Too much time in offices and on busses.

He thought it churlish to complain about his workload, especially in tough times, but it did weigh on him. "Clients have to think you're tough, judges have to think you're tough," he said. "And, especially, prosecutors have to think you're tough. And whether you are or not, you've got to *act* tough."

He was what people used to call a "man's man," somebody you wouldn't mess with, somebody who said little but said it bluntly. Someone with whom you often wound up talking about the top news story of the day, or the sports scores.

Perhaps it was different with his friends? "Friends? I don't have time to make friends." He talked with his siblings, scattered all over the country (their parents had died) every Sunday just after he attended mass, but via conference call.

Though driven, he wasn't entirely like the men of the previous generation. He talked about his family a fair amount. One of those quasi-new breed fathers, he was much warmer and more involved with his kids than his predecessors, but still not as much as he wanted to be or thought he should.

"I'm afraid sometimes," he told me once after considerable prodding, "that I will grow up being a stranger to my kids, like my dad was to me, sort of. I hope that doesn't happen."

So Rob was continuously wondering what his son or daughters were thinking, what they were up to, if they were really okay. It was Judy, he admitted with some envy, who really knew the details of their lives.

Judy loved their stucco-and-timber house with its wide lawn and spacious yard. She, along with a housekeeper, a two-day-a-week gardener, and a decorator, embarked on renovating it, inside and out. Well-tended and tasteful, the property had no visible garbage cans, trash shrubbery, or weeds.

The Cochrans were wealthier than the average household, although $600,000 houses were no longer a rarity in Montclair. But life in their Tudor house was familiarly child-centered. Their SUV and minivan made nearly continuous runs to sporting events, Sunday school, music lessons, sleepovers, and playdates; the garage was filling with mountain bikes, sleds, and skis, the upstairs bedrooms with computers.

Yet apart from the occasional appearance at a weekend sporting event, Rob was around for little of this. "I wouldn't know how to drive to any of these places except the soccer field and the schools," he said. He'd be the first to concede one of the ironies of Montclair life: for all the social upheaval about gender roles and the new structure of families, men still weren't around that much. This was partly economic, of course. It had become expensive to live in Montclair, so despite the many two-career families in town, the men generally earned more and spent more time at it. Even in a town where social change was everywhere evident, some things hadn't changed as much as people liked to think, or hoped.

The reason Rob rose so early was to take his genial, excitable, and perpetually ravenous two-year-old black Labrador for a long romp through the Mills Reservation. This was what Rob called his "contract with the dog": he gave Cherokee one extended walk per day, no matter what, and in return the dog overlooked and forgave his long absences, his reticence, his occasional grumpiness, and other foibles. He was a man, he pointed out, who took contracts seriously; and so, he believed, did his dog.

Rob dearly loved Cherokee—the name materialized while Rob was watching one of his beloved John Wayne westerns on cable—and grinned whenever he looked at him.

Cherokee was, in his eyes, handsome and affectionate; but, especially, he was loyal, a close and intimate presence that could literally be taken for granted—just the kind of friend few men had.

"He'd take a bullet for me," he was fond of saying. The dog, as he described him, was nobly well-bred, steadfast, possessed of a mighty roaming and hunting spirit. In fact, Cherokee's outstanding quality was his affability. He was profoundly goodnatured, although if one drew a cartoon balloon over the dog's head, it would say: "Food!" Cherokee was one of those Labs for whom food was not mere nourishment.

Early histories of this breed recount brutal, unforgiving lives in harsh Canadian climates (Labs are really from Newfoundland, not Labrador). Before being imported to England and bred to look regal, they worked with fishermen, retrieving fish, pulling nets, learning to scavenge and to avoid pickiness about meals. As a result, many Labs will eat anything that remotely resembles food and many things that don't. Montclair vets all had stories about what they'd removed from Labrador stomachs. "They're a smart breed," said Brenda

King, a vet who'd spent many Tuesday mornings—surgery days—opening up Labs to remove
balls, bones, cans, and rocks. "But when it comes
to food, they can be awfully stupid."

Cherokee was such a dog. He had been in her
surgery twice. He would eat virtually anything he
could fit in his mouth. He was always sniffing for
crumbs on the floor, snorkeling through the garbage, inhaling goose droppings at the park, leaping
on people carrying treats or groceries. Cherokee
had gnawed open boxes of cereal and cans of tuna,
eaten oranges whole, even munched through the
family jack-o'-lantern he found propped on the
porch for Halloween.

Barrel-chested and powerfully built, bred to
run hard and hunt, Cherokee would also plunge
headfirst into any body of water, from an ocean to
a mud puddle.

If Rob was a lot of man, Cherokee was a lot of
dog. If Cherokee didn't get his time at Mills, Rob
worried, he might eat through a wall of their home.
Hence his banishment to the laundry room, where,
supplied with knuckle bones, he spent most days
eating or watching for Rob's return, his massive
paws propped against a window as he scanned the
sidewalk, waiting.

Rob leashed Cherokee and took him out to
the Land Cruiser. At this hour, Montclair's
streets—soon to be teeming with vans, school
buses, and kids and parents walking to school—

were stone silent. Yet when Rob pulled into the dark Mills lot, it was nearly full. The eerie scene—cars' headlights, waving flashlights, and barking dogs—felt like the opening of *E.T.*

Half a dozen other Manhattan-bound men with big dogs were already there; two were with giant mastiffs, others with Labs, retrievers, and some energetic mixed breeds. The owners looked disheveled and bleary-eyed in their sweatpants and jeans, and a couple waved at Rob and Cherokee. A dedicated bunch of dog owners, none of them really had to be there. Most people in their situation would have simply walked the dogs around the block or hired someone to do it. But, like Rob, they felt they owed their dogs this much. The dogs, meanwhile, were sniffing and circling and peeing, eager to head out onto the trails.

Rob let Cherokee out of the car and unleashed him, and the dog made a beeline for a large guy in a khaki photographer's vest who shielded his crotch with his hands as Cherokee plowed into him. "Sorry," Rob yelled, as Cherokee nosed the man's pockets none too gently. He got a treat from a vest pocket, then barked for more. Rob apologized again.

These were the early morning regulars; they mustered at 5:00, waited a few minutes for stragglers. Then, at 5:05—they all had trains or buses to catch—Dan, a local TV news producer and the group's unofficial organizer, said, "All right, let's move 'em out," and the men and dogs plunged down the main path. A couple of the guys tried briefly to keep order, but the pack, including Cherokee, was already off into the woods.

Packs like this were part of what was fueling controversy about dogs off-leash at Mills. The sight of a throng of large dogs bounding through the woods terrified some people, and there was some truth to the notion that a group of dogs running loose was really under nobody's control. But at this hour, there was nobody much to scare. The elderly strollers and families with small kids were still at home, and the few other dog people took the pack in stride.

The pace was brisk; usually, Rob said, they did the two-mile trail in less than forty minutes. Few of the groggy men actually knew one another. They sometimes talked about how their dogs were or how the market was doing, but that was about the extent of the conversation.

Dan had organized the group, spotting potential members on his strolls through Montclair parks and inviting people one by one. His own yellow Lab, Streak, was highly social; Dan thought he should have friends.

In fact, that's largely why they walked together, Rob said. Besides the exercise, they all believed their dogs enjoyed the company of other dogs, although after some initial sniffing, most of the dogs paid little attention to the others.

The trails at Mills were also beautifully quiet at this hour, and the men reveled in watching their powerful dogs tear freely through the woods, romping in circles, just being dogs. It had become a rare sight in Montclair.

The Manhattan lights still winked in the distance as the group moved through a clearing, though the skyline grew less distinct as the sky lightened. "Mostly, on these walks, I sort of plan my day," Rob explained later. "At night, when it's just me and Cherokee, it's more of a bonding thing." None of the men seemed much interested in bonding with one another.

As Rob volunteered pointedly, the dog-walking group wasn't for the humans—"It's *not* a men's group or anything like that"—but for the dogs. He couldn't name more than two or three of the regulars.

"Cherokee," he called out. "Yo, Cherokee!" He'd belatedly figured out why experienced dog owners used one- or two-syllable names—much easier to say. After a moment or three, the big Lab came pounding back down the trail to him, then bounded off again into the brush.

Most of the men were toting scoopers or doggie bags, along with flashlights and coffee mugs. This was a responsible, law-abiding crowd, Rob noted, quick to chastise those who didn't clean up after their dogs. "Otherwise, they'll ruin it for all of us." He glossed over the fact that it was illegal for any of them to walk their dogs off-leash in Mills at all.

Cherokee loved this morning ritual, running ahead at top speed, tearing after other dogs or hapless raccoons, always circling back to Rob, though not always precisely when Rob called him.

By 5:45, the group had circled back to the parking lot, the dogs had all been summoned back into the cars, and the group mumbled some hurried goodbyes, then disintegrated. Nobody had the time to admire the sunrise. They'd reconvene the next morning.

The group walk was designed to be maintenance-free, requiring no communication, expense, or coordination, Dan pointed out. People arrived at five, walked, then left. Nobody had to pay dues, print flyers, make phone calls, or bring anything other than dogs or leashes. The sole obligation was to show up.

If somebody didn't, no notification was required or expected. After several weeks or months, a replacement would be invited, and no one ever expected to see the missing parties again.

Back at the house, Rob put a mud-soaked Cherokee in the backyard, tossing him a tennis ball, which Cherokee chased once or twice before losing interest. "I wish he'd go in for chasing balls more," Rob muttered. "Get more exercise that way. Wear him out."

He went upstairs, showered, changed into an expensive navy suit, collected his battered leather briefcase, hugged and kissed his wife, who was just getting up, and headed off to New York to do legal combat. He wished he could take Cherokee to work once in a while, but the building had strict rules about dogs, and it probably wouldn't work out anyway. "Too many bagels and doughnuts around," Rob joked.

When the kids came crashing downstairs, the house grew chaotic, as Judy served breakfast, reviewed plans for rides to lessons and games, backstopped everybody on lunches and backpacks.

Cherokee was allowed to be in the kitchen with the family at breakfast, but he remained detached from this madness. He moved beneath the kitchen table, lapping up crumbs, sometimes lifting his head to help himself to an inviting muffin or piece of toast. The only real connection between the dog and the family was through Rob. Nobody else paid much attention to him, and vice versa. Only Sean, the youngest, said goodbye to Cherokee when he left for the bus.

With the kids dispatched, Judy cleaned up, then returned Cherokee to the yard, since it was a nice day; if it were rainy or cold, he'd be back in the laundry room. "He's happier outside," she said, somewhat apologetically.

The family was well organized and well mannered. Cherokee was the wild one. If there were any dead or disgusting thing out in the woods or on the street, Cherokee could find it, roll in it, eat it. Rob couldn't count the number of times the dog regurgitated something ghastly after a walk. He kept rags, disinfectant, and deodorizing spray in the back of his car and in the laundry room.

Judy was perpetually—and with good reason—worried about her new furniture and expensive carpets, but Rob rather appreciated the dog's wild side.

"I love to see him work out," he said. "It's fun to see a dog run like that. I'd love to go hunting with him, if I had time. If I liked hunting." Montclair wasn't exactly Marlboro Country.

When Cherokee disappeared into the woods after some animal or another dog, Rob grew anxious and called his name, but the dog's "recall" was spotty at best. He always came eventually, but only when he felt like it. When he did come bounding up, he was apt to jump up and plow into Rob or one of the other men at Mills.

These collisions were never aggressive, but they were often startling. Cherokee was a huge slobbery dog with perpetually muddy paws and untrimmed claws. And he was strong. Even on a leash, with Rob struggling to tow him down the sidewalk, working hard to keep him out of the street and out of trouble, he'd been known to leave people doubled over or brushing mud off their clothes.

An orderly and disciplined man, Rob was perpetually apologizing for the dog's unruly behavior. "I should get him trained," he acknowledged. "Maybe one day I will."

Doubtful. The real issue was that thing that contemporary dog owners seem never to have

114

enough of time. "I barely have time to put my pants on," Rob said, let alone spend a half-hour a day on "heel" and "stay." And he wasn't likely to get less busy soon. Behaviorists estimated that it can take up to 2,000 repetitions of a command before a dog really gets it; with Rob's schedule, it could take a year to hit that mark. And who else would do it? Everybody in the household saw Cherokee as Rob's dog and Rob's headache, including Rob.

Judy wasn't a likely candidate. She and Rob had actually negotiated an arrangement—another contract, of sorts—that protected her from too much dog duty.

An urban planner with a Columbia degree, she never particularly wanted the dog. She'd taken a few years off from work for motherhood and household renovations, and had agreed to a new puppy after their previous Lab died because Rob seemed to want one so badly. He promised to assume its care, and Judy knew if he said he would, he would.

She also understood why he needed a dog. "Rob doesn't make close friends, and he doesn't talk much about himself. He really values his time with Cherokee, it's important to him. Sometimes I think he's a little lonely. It's hard for him to make friends in a town like this. With his schedule, it's hard for him to meet people, especially other men.

"I'm not the type to tell my spouse he can or can't do something. We're independent people," she said. "But that doesn't mean I have to be responsible for it. But Rob works so hard, he's under so much pressure, I don't know what he'd do without that dog. He's crazy about him."

So they struck a deal: he got the new dog, but only under certain conditions.

- The dog wasn't allowed upstairs, ever. Cherokee slept in the laundry room, where he could do minimal damage to the evolving renovation with dirty paws, shedding hair, powerful tail (capable of taking out tall lamps with a single wag), or his voracious appetite.
- Judy didn't walk the dog, feed him, or take him to the vet, except in dire emergencies.
- When they entertained, the dog would be kept out of sight. Even Rob didn't want to see his partners, neighbors, or Judy's girlfriends subjected to Cherokee's special paws-on-shoulders greeting.
- The dog didn't go along on family vacations. That one bothered Rob most—he tended to get antsy after a few days alone with the kids—but he agreed. There wasn't enough room in the Land Cruiser for five humans and Cherokee anyway.

On the whole, Judy was good-natured about life with Cherokee, retaining the requisite sense of humor. "It's a look," she liked to say when she found trash strewn about the kitchen. She believed in give-and-take, an important trait in any person

116

living with a dog lover. But she wasn't about to administer training sessions.

What about the kids, then? Couldn't one of them work to tame the obstreperous Cherokee?

Not really. Friends came and went, the phone rang continuously, the car-pooling and driving to lessons and activities challenged even an urban planner's organizational skills. The older daughter was about to go off to college, her sister was deeply enmeshed in just about every sport offered at the high school, and you couldn't pry the youngest kid off the Net with a crowbar. Montclair parents often joked that their children had pulled off a nonviolent coup d'état. They were in control.

Rob shook his head at the very idea. "I learned my lesson about that. Truth is, I don't trust the kids with the dog anyway. I'm not one of those parents who got the dog for the kids. I got the dog for me."

To make sure Cherokee didn't languish all day in his absence, Rob hired a professional dog walker. At least a score are active in Montclair, drumming up business with ads in the local weekly, with flyers passed around at pet shops and vets' offices, by word of mouth.

Allie Shea was popular and trusted in Rob's neighborhood, and he paid her to walk Cherokee every weekday around noon, plus occasional nights and weekends if Rob was busy. Paying her $15 for a half-hour walk partly assuaged his guilt at being away so much.

Shea was a cheerful, experienced dog lover, careful to praise Cherokee's good nature, but she clearly found it hard to handle this dog, who half-obeyed Rob and completely ignored everyone else. Like Rob, Shea called Cherokee a "big lug," but with somewhat less affection. Still, she gave him a bit of a workout that lasted until Rob came home for the evening walk.

After dinner one weekday evening, Rob and Cherokee were heading out for their nightly "bonding" walk. Cherokee had just downed his own dinner, his second meal of the day.

"The vet says he needs to lose some weight," Rob said, "but what can you do? He's so hungry I can't cut back."

Once Rob took the leash from its hook, Cherokee was all over him, jumping, prancing, knocking a small wastepaper basket onto the kitchen floor.

Rob looked exhausted after a long day that included the walk through Mills, a nasty commute, meetings with clients, a court appearance, and negotiations with federal prosecutors over a fraud case. He wasn't really up for a stroll around the block with boisterous, cranked-up Cherokee, but he kept his word.

"Easy, big guy, easy," Rob murmured, trying to leash the big guy. "Cut it out now." Annoyance was creeping into his voice. He'd managed to slip the lead onto the dog's collar when Cherokee lunged toward the back screen door and pushed it open, jerking Rob along with him.

"Hey! Hey!" Rob shouted as the dog pulled out onto the sidewalk. "He loves to walk." Exasperated, he was also amused by the dog's enthusiasm.

Usually, Rob said, he enjoyed these nightly strolls, and perhaps he meant it, but walks with this dog didn't seem like that much fun. Cherokee was a challenge, even by Labrador standards. He pulled toward a bush, then back toward the sidewalk. He sniffed something up ahead and tugged Rob nearly off his feet. Twice in a week, Cherokee had dragged Rob a few feet off the curb and into the street, chasing after something.

A passing neighbor, heading home from the New York bus, didn't notice the pair in the dusk until Cherokee startled him by leaping up. Rob, who hadn't seen the man in the shadows, was equally surprised. "Jesus!" the guy yelled. Rob apologized and then gently chided the dog. "Settle down, will ya, big guy? Don't go jumping up on people." When Ellie the dachshund hopped up to greet people, she barely reached their calves. Cherokee plowed into people's chests and stomachs, and he weighed about ninety pounds more than Ellie.

A dog trainer would have offered one of those easier-said-than-done sayings, like "You walk the dog; don't let the dog walk you." But on these forays, Cherokee did the walking.

Like many people with untrained dogs, Rob had gotten into the habit of yelling commands to get Cherokee's attention, and then, when he was ignored, repeating them loudly. So their walk was punctuated with angry exhortations: "Cherokee! Cherokee! Damnit, Cherokee! Come! Come! Come here! Sit! Sit now! Sit! Lie down! Bad boy! Bad!"

This sort of interspecies pairing was epidemic in Montclair: on the one hand, a person who was obviously crazy about a dog but, without training, unable to communicate with it effectively, and, on the other, a dog who seemed oblivious but was in fact probably learning all the wrong lessons. Dogs often crave attention, even in the form of yells; by shouting ignored commands at their dogs, owners frequently reinforce the very behaviors they are trying to stop.

He really couldn't bear to get tough with "the big lug," Rob admitted as they zigzagged down the sidewalk, the human listing at a forty-five-degree angle to hold on to the canine. "I'm not stupid. I know what the trainers say. 'You've got to show them who's boss.'"

Actually, the literature on dog training is filled with all sorts of divergent opinions. Dog training has a panoply of factions and philosophies. Some trainers argue that dogs are best taught by rewarding the desired behaviors with praise or food. Some believed that the pack theory applies to dogs, but not generally to their relationships with humans.

Men like Rob, however, tended to favor the more traditional approach: Dogs had to be shown who was boss, period. He chuckled at so-called positive training techniques, deriding them as "touchy-feely" nonsense. "My dad would have gotten a yuk out of that," he muttered. Cherokee, he added, "has a mind of his own. One of the things I love about him. I don't want a robot."

He was reluctant, he said, to crush that streak of independence. As he spoke, he gave the impression he knew what that felt like. He couldn't bear to get tough with his dog.

The truth was that Cherokee didn't appear either independent or defiant; he merely seemed to be poorly trained, with no clue that Rob was even speaking to him, let alone grasping what he wanted him to do. He was doing what some trainers call "blowing the owner off." He rarely made eye contact with Rob, except when something was going on related to food or walking.

Despite Rob's deep affection, he hadn't built a solid relationship with his dog. There was more attachment on the human side of the equation than the canine one. Cherokee didn't appear to focus on Rob, or to take Rob's instructions seriously. Adrift, almost allergic to the many commands that were continually being shouted at him, to no particular effect, the dog seemed a bit of a doofus, disconnected from people—even, at times, from Rob.

Since Cherokee loved food so much, one way Rob could have trained him to come, lie down, and walk properly was to use treats to reward him. If made to lie down when people approached (and given a treat), he might stop jumping up on passersby. But, Rob said, "I don't want the dog to do things for food. I want him to do things because of his relationship with me. I want him to obey me."

Thus, a big and energetic Labrador found himself in a catch-22: he was expected to do things for the sake of a relationship he wasn't fully given the chance to have. In one sense, these two were deeply attached. In another, Cherokee was set up to fail.

Anyway, Rob argued, carrying treats around seemed indulgent, as well as a pain. He thought it weird that I'd used everything from beef jerky to frozen tortellini to train one of my recalcitrant border collies.

"I didn't get a special diet when I was a kid," he recalled. "We ate what was on the table, or my dad would send us to bed. So I'm not carrying around gourmet treats for a dog."

Kelly, Rob's first Lab, was an animal he'd loved deeply and had owned for twelve years. Then, one day, Sean left the backyard gate open after school—this was four years ago—and Kelly dashed into the street and got hit by a car. Rob made it back from the city to the vet's office shortly before the dog died.

"I felt horrible, and not only for the dog," he told me one evening after his walk with Cherokee. "My son still has nightmares about seeing the dog hit in the street like that. He felt so guilty."

But what about Rob? How did he take that loss?

He looked down at the floor.

"Seeing Kelly dead on the vet's table . . . I just can't describe it, I don't have words for it. It was like getting hit on the head with an anvil.

"And I was in the middle of a trial. You can't get up and tell the judge or your client that you're about to burst into tears because your goddamned dog got hit by a car. But, jeez, that hit me hard. Really hard."

The intensity in his voice was surprising, a level of emotion he rarely permitted himself to express. The pain was all over his face.

The relationship with Cherokee was different from the start. "Kelly was the family dog, the dog I got for the kids. Judy met the breeder through a friend of ours and the kids were screaming for a puppy, and almost everybody falls for that. I loved that dog—she was sweet, slept on the foot of our bed the whole time we lived in Michigan, then Brooklyn, while I was getting started in my law career. Judy didn't mind too much."

But Cherokee was different. Cherokee was his dog all the way. He found the breeder; he drove to North Carolina by himself and brought the puppy home; he housebroke him and began taking him on the daily walks through Mills.

"And things are different for me now," he added. "I wouldn't want to use the word 'lonely,' but the kids more and more have their own lives, and Judy has her own life . . ."

So, would he describe Cherokee as a friend?

"Oh, sure. I'd say a best friend," he responded quickly. "And in a way, much more than that."

Rob seemed to instantly regret saying so, especially when I wondered what he meant. What exactly was "more than that"?

He looked uncomfortable.

"He may not always look it, but he's a sensitive guy," Rob often said of his dog, much as a doting admirer might describe the star football player nobody thought was all that bright. He thought Cherokee loyal, courageous. "I know if someone came after me on our walks, he'd have to kill this dog to get to me." He'd often told his dog walker that Cherokee would sacrifice his life if Rob were in danger, and Allie joked back that he'd better pray the evildoers weren't armed with hot dogs. But to Rob, Cherokee had the heart of a lion.

The second time I asked what "more than a best friend" meant, he said he hadn't really given it much attention and couldn't answer. Pressed again a week later, he said, "You know, I've been thinking about it. Ask me in a few weeks."

It was almost two months before Rob really tried to respond. It was a sticky spring night after Cherokee had knocked over the backyard garbage can and eaten a cardboard container of week-old take-out chicken. Rob didn't even bother going to the vet's anymore for mishaps like this unless Cherokee looked gravely ill or had eaten something with jagged edges.

And, sure enough, Cherokee was fine; he'd

rolled over on his back and dozed off on the Oriental carpet in the den. Rob sat in a faded leather chair, his favorite; Judy was puttering around the kitchen—we heard pots-and-pans clatter—and the three kids were upstairs. Battle sounds, from Sean's new Play Station, drifted down the stairs.

The scene conjured up suburban America at its prosperous, domestic best: successful Dad returned from work, busy and competent Mom at home not because she had to be but because she wanted to be, three healthy and happy kids, beautiful dog by its master's side.

It was not the sort of household Rob had grown up in back in Cleveland.

"I am grateful to my parents," Rob offered. "They were poor, uneducated people and they sent all of us to college. My father ran a plumbing supply store and he worked like a dog; he was never at home. When he could, he'd take a day here and there to take me or my brothers to a ball game, or maybe all of us to the circus, but those were rare occasions."

It was a respectful relationship, but hardly a close one. "I'm not sure we ever had a long, one-on-one conversation in my life. I'm not sure I know how to have one. It wasn't that my dad was an SOB. He wasn't; he'd do anything for us. He just didn't like to talk much. And he was tough—oh, man, was he tough! If you messed up, you didn't leave your room for a week, and if it kept up, that belt would come out. And nobody called it abuse, either. It's not the way I raise my kids, you understand—I'd never touch any of them in anger. It's just the way my dad knew. He'd had worse done to him."

Cherokee rolled farther over, his feet splayed in the air, and Rob thoughtfully scratched his stomach with his shoe. I asked if his parents still lived in Cleveland.

Just his mother, he said. His father had died, of cancer, five years ago. "I spent the last month of my father's life at his bedside. I took off from work; my mom really needed me there. I'm the oldest, you know. And all those days, my dad and I never said a word about what was happening, and I knew better than to raise it. Nothing would have made him more uncomfortable. So he just stopped breathing one night as I was sitting there, and I never said goodbye." Rob was staring straight ahead, his voice composed but quiet.

Now, however different his elegant home, his professional career, "I guess I know I'm like my father," Rob said, "in that, basically, I work. I'm the breadwinner. And I'm like him in that I adore my kids, but I don't *talk* to my kids about things. I should, but you know, it's hard to do."

He stared down at Cherokee, stretched out by his chair, uncharacteristically calm. "I think with this dog, I appreciate the fact that we can't speak to each other. There's no pressure to, so I don't feel guilty. Whatever we feel, we just feel."

It's impossible to be around men and dogs for

any length of time—and I've been around a lot of them—without seeing some differences in the ways men and women relate to dogs.

Both men and women see human-style emotions in their dogs and attribute to them all sorts of traits, thoughts, and feelings that dogs probably aren't capable of. The dog as blank canvas: the image we choose to paint, or need to paint, often emerging from the corners of our own lives.

But many women have told me—and much research echoes this notion—that they see dogs as being emotionally supportive: their dogs "understand" them better than anyone, and love them "no matter what." One veterinary-association survey showed that women are much more likely to confide their problems to their dogs, or speak to them regularly about "important" matters.

Men, it appeared to me after following people and dogs around Montclair for months, sometimes seemed drawn to dogs precisely because they *couldn't* speak. This wordlessness left them freer to see relationships the way they wanted them to be, wished they were. Cherokee didn't ask for intimate emotional conversations about the relationship, and never would.

Men, who sometimes struggle to form lasting friendships, are more likely to see a dog as a pal or buddy. Like Rob, they often have action relationships with their dogs: they like to do things with them—hunt, jog, walk, retrieve, wrestle, drive around town. Women, in my experience, tend to have more verbal and emotionally complex relationships with their dogs, and are more likely to have and imagine conversations with them.

However bumptious or ill-behaved Cherokee appeared to an outsider, it didn't really matter to Rob. The dog was giving Rob something more important than obedience, something that mattered even if he wasn't aware of it or of its complex and distant origins.

But what was it exactly?

As successful as he was, surrounded by his wife and kids, there was a disconnectedness about Rob—from the town he was away from all day, from his children, from the society beyond his work and home. He had no close friends, not even the dog guys at Mills. He had no interests and little time to pursue any. In some ways, Cherokee filled that void.

As veterinarian Victoria Voith writes in a 1985 veterinary journal: "If we are genetically predisposed to becoming attached to other people, particularly our children, and if animals exhibit many of the same characteristics that cause our attachment to other people, it is easy to see why people become attached to pets and, in many respects, behave and feel towards them as though the animal were a child. People know a dog is a dog, but can feel about it as though it *were* a person."

So, after weeks of my badgering him to talk

about his attachment to Cherokee, Rob finally came up with an explanation: "You know why I love this dog?" he said. "Because he never asks me questions like that."

CHAPTER 5

THE DIVORCED DOGS CLUB

On a rainy Friday evening, a mud-soaked group of five women and their dogs trooped from Mills Reservation into Rachel Goldner's house for the not-quite-weekly meeting of the Divorced Dogs Club. Soon the women were lounging around the living room with cups of tea or glasses of merlot—dogs dozing in various corners—and cracking themselves up by concocting a list: all the qualities that made their dogs helpful, loyal, supportive, and otherwise unlike certain other species one might mention.

"They don't give a damn what you wear," said Rachel, leading off.

"They see you at your worst and love you just the same," piped up Carolyn.

"You don't have to convince them that you understand them," Sally added. "You don't have to make time for them. They appreciate the time they get."

"Chester always wants to rent the same video I want to rent," was Janice's offering. She meant her black Lab. "That was not true of Gerald." She meant her ex-husband.

"They don't lie," Rachel said.

"And they don't fall in love with other people," added Cynthia, jumping in out of turn. "And they're not insecure about their masculinity."

There were, it turned out, many advantages to living with dogs. They went to the bathroom quickly—and outside. They were happy to spend holidays with the women's trying relatives. They didn't leave dirty clothes and smelly shoes lying around. They didn't stare at televised football games on beautiful fall afternoons.

"They have no agendas," Sally said.

"Except feed me and love me," said Janice.

"And they don't want to have sex with you at strange times!" Cynthia blurted out, as the rest of the group shrieked.

"Well, that's probably a good thing." Rachel was laughing so hard she had to set down her wineglass.

"Or maybe not," said Cynthia, to more howls.

Carolyn raised her hand, then laughed at herself for acting as if she were in high school. "Amen to that. But I wouldn't forget something else . . . Talk about empowerment all you want, but sometimes being a woman alone is a bit scary. And these guys, well, they protect us. I think this guy"—she reached down to scratch her Dalmatian, Sharpton, behind the ears, and he wagged his tail and licked her hand—"would do anything for me. I might be kidding myself, but I think he would."

"And aren't we forgetting one of the biggest

things of all?" asked Janice, causing the group to quiet down and listen. "They don't leave!"

The list grew longer, and it wasn't, of course, entirely a joke. For all the wisecracks, these women hated being divorced; they'd felt emotionally mauled by what they'd endured. Divorce had become so commonplace that it was hard for other people to grasp how wrenching it was—unless you were going through it yourself. All of them *had* gone through it, and their dogs had made a huge difference.

The members who'd dubbed their group the Divorced Dogs Club didn't see the dogs as surrogate mates; they loved them as dogs and they kept on loving them as dogs as they tried to move on with their lives.

Sometimes the Divorced Dogs Club met at a park; once they visited a big discount pet-supply store. But tonight, as most often, the group assembled at Rachel's house, a spectacular modern bilevel that hung over Highland Avenue on the affluent ridge that offered a hypnotic view of Manhattan's skyline.

It might be the last time the group could meet in that gorgeous living room or barbecue on her patio. Rachel, a fit, elegant, gray-haired former school psychologist in her fifties, had just finalized her divorce. She and her ex-husband, the CEO of a successful sporting-goods chain, had agreed to sell the house and split the proceeds down the middle. Divorce, one of the women said, was like an avalanche. Once it began, it moved everything and everybody in its path.

Rachel was stricken about leaving the airy, glass-walled home she and Glenn had built, where they'd raised their two children. It was a lovelier home than she'd ever dreamed of having. But she and the rest of the group were otherwise pleased with her settlement, which would give her and her feisty little pug, Aviva, security for life. Thanks to her excellent, no-holds-barred lawyer, Glenn had gotten eaten alive, Rachel said. And he deserved to be, after carrying on a secret affair for three years. It was a guilt settlement. "He felt bad about me, and just wanted me to go away," Rachel said. "So I will." There were approving murmurs and expressions of support.

Between chats, Rachel was moving back and forth through the sliding glass doors to the patio, where she was preparing chicken breasts for the canine members of the club, who'd gathered expectantly around the gas grill. Besides Aviva, Rachel's three-year-old pug and monarch of all she surveyed, there was Chester, the good-hearted black Lab who belonged to Janice, a homemaker and fanatic jogger divorced two years before. And Sharpton the Dalmatian, the "biracial" member of the group, whose owner, Carolyn, a freelance business reporter, was in the midst of reasonably amicable but still sad divorce proceedings.

Gusty, a rescued greyhound from a racing complex in Florida, the group's shyest and most skittish member, belonged to Cynthia, an attorney who practiced in Morristown. Cynthia and her husband had two children, teenagers, and they'd fought over every paragraph of the kids' custody and support agreement. But they'd battled more bitterly over the dog than anything else. Cynthia was proud that she hadn't lost custody of Gusty to her ex.

The fifth member of the group was Sally, an emergency-room physician who worked nights at the University of Dentistry and Medicine in Newark and therefore could only make meetings sporadically. Her standard poodle Christie, hyperactive and untrained, loved chasing balls and leaping onto people, not necessarily in that order.

It was Janice who'd come up with the idea for the Divorced Dogs Club. She was walking Chester one evening at Mills Reservation, maybe a hundred yards up the hill from the patio where Rachel now stood barbecuing, when he took off after a squirrel or a raccoon and they ran into Rachel and Aviva coming up a path from the house. They were two different women—Janice was fifteen years younger, lean from running, prone to spending her days in sneakers and sweats—with more in common than they might have thought.

"We started doing dog talk with each other. You know—'How old is he?' 'How did you train her?' 'What does he eat?' 'Can you believe we can love a dog this much?'—and next thing, we were having

134

a cup of coffee here. Chester and Aviva really hit if off, and so did we."

Each sensed the other was going through a split-up. Rachel was convinced that she could spot her sister divorcees, even in the supermarket. "It's a frayed, haunted, slightly panic-stricken look," she said. "We knew right away. We started bashing our ex-husbands, and that's when we discovered that we each had a divorce dog."

Meaning, Janice explained, a dog acquired specifically to help them through their marital troubles and the lonely aftermath. She got Chester "right after my husband told me he didn't want to live with me anymore, that he wanted to be with somebody else."

Rachel laughed and interrupted. "I couldn't believe it—my husband used almost the exact same words. The next week, I went out and found a breeder and told him I wanted the toughest pug in his next litter." Not such an uncommon impulse, it turned out.

Cynthia, a chunky, fast-talking brunette in her early forties, with cropped hair and a lot of jewelry, knew Janice from an exercise class. "She knew what I'd been through, and I said I wanted in. I came for a couple of trial walks and meetings. Then we met Carolyn walking up at Mills and we all liked each other. We were also impressed by Sharpton because he growled at men but not women."

"Aw, c'mon," pleaded Carolyn. "That's not true, not exactly."

Gusty was a different sort of divorce dog. Cynthia and her ex adopted the delicate greyhound together, "but we fought over him more than anything, so he was, to me, the symbol of our divorce. My husband didn't have an affair. He's not that lucky. He's just a—"

"Ah-ah-ah," clucked Rachel, casting a cautionary eye toward me. "Let's be positive. We don't need to air our dirty laundry here."

Cynthia gave her a grateful nod. No dirty laundry.

Everyone here had been alternately shocked, saddened, embarrassed, or infuriated—sometimes all of the above—during their breakups. They had each instinctively turned to a dog for help—and then to other divorcing women with dogs. There were meetings when the anger spilled over and people listened, sympathetically, but for the most part they worked to keep one another's spirits up.

"We should call ourselves the Ya-Ya Dog Club," Rachel suggested. She took the chicken breasts off the grill with a long fork and Janice cut them up and distributed them. "All dogs are not created equal," she said.

Chester reinforced this point. The size of a small moose, he got about a third of the chicken, which he nearly inhaled, as did Sharpton. Aviva the pug got the smallest chunk and retreated into a distant corner of the patio to work on it; it would take her a while. The nearly emaciated-looking Gusty got a slightly larger portion, which he hoarded rather than ate. The happy sounds of slurping and chomping wafted across the patio.

The women fed themselves next; on busy nights it was Chinese takeout, but today Rachel had put together a pasta dish and a salad. Drinks were at a bar by the kitchen door. Wine was about as far as anybody went, although Cynthia had indulged in Scotch a couple of times when she was feeling especially blue. They settled back in the living room with plates and glasses to talk.

The members of the DDC were ironic as well as self-aware. They thought the very idea of their group hilarious, not to be taken too seriously. "My son can't *believe* that I'm in a 'divorced dogs' group," Cynthia said, laughing. "He says it's the lamest, most pathetic thing he's ever heard in his life. I told him he couldn't possibly understand. He is, after all, a man."

Nobody in the group wanted to broadcast the existence of the club. It was just too ripe for ridicule, and they feared seeming pathetic—although one woman had mentioned it to her vet (who tipped me off). "You wouldn't want to tell the other lawyers in your firm that you're heading off to the Divorced Dogs Club," Cynthia laughed. "Sorry, no offense, but it just wouldn't elevate your standing with the guys."

The other person in town who knew was the owner of Montclair Pet and Feed Supply. "You cannot keep secrets from your pet-store owner," Rachel said gravely. "He knows what kind of treats we waste money on, and what kind of doggie-poop bags we use. It's too intimate a relationship."

Although no one said so directly, there was a sense, an understanding, that the group was probably ephemeral. To be alone with a dog for companionship was not a status any of them necessarily wanted to maintain for very long. But the club, now in its sixth month, still mattered.

"We all need some support, at least for now," Cynthia said, leaning over to stroke and reassure the trembling Gusty, then turning to her own dinner. "We all have gotten more from dogs than from certain people . . ." The trick, she pointed out, was to remember that ultimately, there *were* humans, even men, as trustworthy and affectionate as dogs. "The only problem is, I haven't found too many."

The meetings generally lasted no more than two hours. Besides food and drink, there was dog talk—about vet visits, eating problems, fights with other dogs, guilt over using boarding kennels. Gusty was seeing a trainer to help her overcome her shyness. Chester was recovering from surgery after eating a tennis ball.

And there was some divorce talk. They talked about how confusing, isolated, and strange their lives had become. Kids were disturbed; old friends melted away; DVDs replaced movie theaters; there were more meals at home; new friends were hard to make. They felt financial pressure and fears about the future, about growing older alone, about how their kids were faring. In suburban towns like Montclair, where life centered on families, single or divorced women sometimes felt invisible, anachronisms and outcasts in a universe of couples with kids. "Maybe if I became a soccer coach," joked Cynthia, the bluntest member.

They talked, trying not to lapse into angry harangues, about the messy, expensive, often confrontational business of divorce itself. "People don't realize it's just the beginning of a disruptive ordeal that goes on for years," Janice explained. "Paperwork, negotations, lawyers, agreements. Yuk. It really wears you down." Sometimes, despite the attempts to stay upbeat, the pain in the room was palpable.

But the Divorced Dogs Club was as clearly defined by what it wasn't as by what it was: it wasn't, everyone agreed, a therapy group. Most of its members were seeing real therapists, or had at some point. They didn't expect or want such soul-baring here. In fact, few of the group's relationships extended much beyond dog walking and these meetings. What they shared was dogs. Dogs were working for them, helping them get through, providing what they perceived as unconditional love, loyalty, and companionship.

There were probably too many disparities for deep friendships to form. Carolyn, for example, was in her early thirties but seemed barely older than a college kid. She was the only African-American in the club, and her close friends tended, likewise, to be young and black and from newly hip Brooklyn, whence she had just moved.

Rachel, the eldest and the closest thing the group had to a leader, was active in Jewish charities. She traveled frequently to Florida, where she had a lot of family, and was almost always tanned. With longtime roots in Montclair, she went to half a dozen meetings a week and treasured a bevy of old and dear friends.

Everybody loved Cynthia's smart-ass, combative style, but she acknowledged that being "edgier" than the other women in the group also meant she wasn't particularly good at making friends or building a new social life. Besides, she worked long hours, and when she wasn't, she tried to spend as much time as possible with her teenaged daughter and son. The problem was, "they don't especially want to spend a lot of time with me." She knew that was natural for kids their age, even healthy, but it still left her feeling lonely, "and, frankly, a bit useless." Gusty, on the other hand, never wanted to go to the mall instead of spending the day with her.

Sally—frizzy-haired, makeup free, indifferent to fashion—conceded that doctors were like cops: they tended to be most comfortable with one another. Her work, in a Newark ER, where she saw every kind of mayhem, was so intense that she often felt disconnected from "normal" people.

Christie had really been her husband's dog, but after the split he moved back into the city. So the poodle was left to her—another variant of a divorce dog—even though she wasn't really a dog person and relied on a dog walker to keep Christie from bouncing off the walls.

Janice, meanwhile, felt awkward about being a housewife in the company of high-powered career women. But to her mind she was doing the crucial work, raising two kids.

"Amen to that," said Rachel, whose kids were already launched.

Even their divorces had been very different. Rachel had been crushed when her husband announced he was in love with someone else. She'd thought her marriage, which had lasted more than three decades, was invulnerable. "I expected Glenn and me to be buried together," she told me once. "Now I have no idea where I'll be buried, or who with. That keeps haunting me. I guess it will be with Aviva. Didn't some ancient tribes bury their dogs with the dead? What a good idea: my companion on this side, and on the other." Nearing sixty, she doubted—although the other women told her she was wrong—that she would ever have another serious relationship with a man. "I'm not even a hundred percent sure that I want one. Maybe I'll just be Auntie Mame, sailing around in style, visiting my children and one day my grandchildren, popping up with Aviva here and there."

Cynthia's divorce had been particularly brutal, hand-to-hand court combat every inch of the way, a draining culmination to a tumultuous fifteen-year relationship.

Sally lost her husband to her medical career, she sighed: he wanted someone more available, more nurturing, less exhausted. Now Sally was becoming interested in a colleague, a physician at her hospital who was lively, simpatico, and female. If that happened, Rachel joked, the club—such diversity!—could run for city council and win.

Carolyn, sleekly stylish in cascading braids and body-skimming shirts and pants, had only recently moved to town with her husband, a white reporter for *The Wall Street Journal*, because it was known as a haven for interracial couples. They got Sharpton (a humorous nod to the black activist, Reverend Al Sharpton) as a prelude to having kids. She thought Montclair lived up to its reputation as a tolerant, culturally sophisticated place, but her husband "simply freaked out" at the thought of moving into the deeply mortgaged middle class, had a "meltdown," and moved back to Brooklyn. She wondered why he hadn't thought about mortgages before they uprooted themselves. He also filed for divorce shortly afterward.

Since he'd never really talked to her about what had happened, she still wasn't quite sure how her life fell apart so abruptly. "I must have missed some major signs," she said, soft-spoken and reflective. "But I sure don't know what they were. Sharpton was more his dog, initially; he was the one who wanted him. But after he left, the dog and I bonded like Crazy Glue."

Carolyn seemed the loneliest member of the group. She freelanced from home, so she had no office colleagues. She hadn't been in Montclair long enough to find a community.

"Honestly, I don't want to be married to a dog," she said, "but I can't imagine what I would have done without Sharpton. He's my shadow. He keeps my heart going, you know what I mean? He sleeps on the bed, cuddles up with me. We go for long walks together. I don't want to be apart from him now. I miss Julian a lot; I still love him. Part of me thinks he'll wake up and snap out of this, but I'm beginning to accept reality. I just can't tell you what this damned dog has meant to me."

Chester came lumbering over and gave Carolyn a big, wet lick on the cheek. Typical.

Chester was the anchor of the dog group, in a way. The other dogs deferred to him because of his gentleness and size (except for Aviva, who growled him away from her food or toys), and the women appreciated his affectionate Lab nature. At meetings, he moved in a continuous circle, dispensing licks, receiving hugs, scarfing up stray crumbs.

At one meeting, they voted Chester "Man of the Year," because of his outstanding qualities as a dog and as a male, awarding him a steak to take home.

"He is loyal, sweet, empathetic, supportive, and honest," Janice said with pride. "Everything a man should be . . ."

"And ain't always," said Cynthia.

In fact, a study under way at a major U.S. veterinary school was finding that more than half the married women in its sample told researchers that they got more emotional support from their dogs than from their husbands. (In March 2001, *The New York Times* reported on a similar survey with almost identical findings.) Their dogs understood them better than some members of their families, they said. More than 80 percent believed their dogs loved them "unconditionally" and would be loyal to them "no matter what." About half said they couldn't really say the same for their spouses.

Janice confided that one group member—nobody would say who—after a particularly nasty conversation with her ex, had suggested having the dogs go outside and pee on his photo.

But Chester had refused, making them all see, said Janice (she was only half-kidding), that bitterness and anger were fruitless, even unhealthy. "He has a larger role here," Rachel said solemnly. "He reminds us that all men aren't bad."

For all these differences, the comfort level in the club was high; the women were at ease with one another. "It's come to mean a lot to me," Rachel said. "Here's a group of terrific women and their dogs, and we're all in the same boat. I don't feel so weird." It was difficult to imagine a group of recently divorced men forming a similar group, with dogs or without.

Such stories reflected the idea of a dog as a new kind of transitional comfort figure, a source of emotional commitment that could help somebody through a painful passage. But if the Divorced Dogs members got enormous support from their dogs, they were also seeking support from humans, from one another, aware of what dogs could do and what they couldn't.

There are inherent dangers for dogs in their new work. Many studies look at how people turn to dogs when they need emotional support but few concern themselves with how the dogs fare in this role. If dogs are social parasites, manipulating humans by showing human-like emotions, the relationship nevertheless remains unequal. The dogs don't get to agree, see therapists, or look for other work. The humans hold all the cards.

In some cases, people have such impossibly high emotional expectations of their pets that they can't help being disappointed. Dogs may be asked to do things dogs can't do, or to have feelings they can't have. But the women of the Divorced Dogs group had impressive clarity about this: they were in trouble, they needed help, and they understood that their dogs could provide some but not all of it. Their ultimate goal was not to depend on dogs for their emotional needs. What these women most wanted was families with partners, a return to a normal footing, having someone to love who could talk back.

The dogs, it was understood, were just filling in. During a period of vulnerability in the women's lives, their dogs were doing one of the things dogs definitely can do, providing loving and secure attachment.

Cynthia pointed out that Gusty was the only creature she could tolerate coming into the bathroom while she was there, or seeing her with her hair rolled up in a towel. It was okay for Gusty to be around when she struggled to fit into last year's clothes. These were things she didn't want her kids to see, let alone a man.

"Gusty follows me from room to room," she said. "He wants to be with me, I'm not forcing him. That's nice for any dog owner, but right now it's especially important, because I have to rebuild that sense of trust. I have to find the faith that some man will want to be with me, and that I can trust him. The dogs keep the nurturing part of us alive, I think."

These women knew—from books, from therapists, from one another—that they'd go through periods of anger, loneliness, depression, disorientation, inactivity. A dog, they thought, could help them survive it.

"And we were right," Janice had concluded. "Sometimes, you're so depressed at the mess you find yourself in that you don't have the energy you need to be with your kids. You just can't give in to it. A lot of people tell me they don't have dogs because they don't want to take that walk at eleven o'clock on a snowy night. But one of the reasons I have a dog is so that I *do* have to get up and take that walk three or four times a day, and it's good for me."

It's good for a lot of people. John Archer, the British psychologist who theorized that dogs are among the world's most skillful social parasites, wrote in 1996 in the journal *Evolution and Human Behavior* that it's the social arrangements of modern Western societies that drive the growing bonds humans forge with pets. Mobility and divorce have gnawed away at the extended family, so family units are growing smaller. The trend toward smaller households has reached its logical and inevitable conclusion: more people live alone.

"There are indications of greater attachment to pets among those with fewer close human ties, such as single and divorced people," Archer wrote. This is especially true, he found, in comparison to families with children. Women living alone are significantly lonelier than those living with pets. Archer found no evidence that the people who turned to dogs were deficient in forming human attachments, but considerable evidence that people living alone do form especially strong attachments to dogs and other pets.

As far back as 1962, the kind of acceptance the Divorced Dogs Club has lately found was already the subject of analytical study. Writing in the *American Journal of Psychiatry*, psychiatrist A. Siegel explained why dogs could be effective in certain kinds of therapy: "The animal does not judge but offers a feeling of intense loyalty . . . It is not frightening or demanding, nor does it expose its master to the ugly strain of constant criticism. It provides its owner with the chance to feel important."

Pat Sable addressed the same subject in 1995 in the *Journal of the National Association of Social Workers*. The presence of pets increases feelings of security and self-worth and reduces loneliness and isolation, Sable wrote, especially "during separations or transitions such as spousal bereavement."

Dogs have been doing a lot of this therapeutic work in Montclair and elsewhere. "We all should have gone to my neighbors' therapist," joked Cynthia.

Which turned out to be an important story. If dogs could help people through their marital crises, as these women intuitively believed and various psychologists and mental health specialists agreed, could they also act to protect couples from the fate of the people in the Divorced Dog Club? Cynthia had told them the story of her neighbors, Steve and Melanie Cabral, who later agreed to talk with me.

The Cabrals—she was an aspiring novelist; he was a film editor for a Manhattan-based production company—had been married for three years, and after some problems adjusting were somewhat surprised to find themselves in a therapist's office for "a bit" of marriage counseling.

It wasn't that they didn't love each other or weren't fully committed, Melanie was eager to point out. But they had some things to sort out.

"I zigged where Steve zagged," was the way she put it, looking back on that awkward period. They had different interests. At home after work, he was perpetually watching a DVD or a sports broadcast; she was something of a physical fitness nut who liked to hike and ski and ran three miles every day. She was social and wanted to meet new people; he was an introvert.

None of this was supposed to matter much, because they expected soon to be caught up in caring for the good-sized family they both wanted. They'd bought a three-bedroom Victorian "starter" house a few blocks away from the high school, with a fenced yard big enough for a swing set and a sandbox. Then, trying to become pregnant, they got the sad news that they faced difficult fertility problems.

It wasn't clear whether they would be able to have a biological child, or whether they might have to adopt. It would take a couple of stressful and expensive years to find out. In their confusion and dismay, they found a therapist who met with each of them individually, then together for the third and fourth sessions. They were taken aback when, toward the end of an hour that had covered a lot of ground, the therapist tossed out: "Have you thought about a dog?"

That was all she said, just a question, and then the session ended.

But they couldn't stop talking about the idea when they got home. "It was like a bell went off," Melanie said. "A dog could hold us together until we figured out how to have a kid. It was something for both of us to love, something to love us, something to bind us."

Three weeks later, they drove to the North Shore Animal Shelter on Long Island before dawn—so they'd be first in line when the shelter opened—to pick up a two-year-old golden retriever named Lola whom they'd spotted on Petfinder.com.

"Talk about love at first sight," said Steve, as Lola herself nuzzled his hand, then jumped up onto the sofa where they were sitting. "From the first, she was crazy about us. You could see it."

Perhaps their therapist had in mind what Dorothy Burlingham wrote about in her book *Twins:* a deeply rooted, universal need for faithful love and unswering devotion, an attempt to find it through an uncritical, understanding, always loving creature. It was no longer possible to remember the number of times I'd heard someone say that a dog loved him or her instantly, totally, completely. If this perception wasn't always literally true, it did often appear to be very important to the person who spoke of it.

When Lola landed on their doorstep, the dog was a mess—hyper, overweight, untrained. She lunged and pulled on a leash, obeyed no commands, jumped up on furniture and people, ate anything that wasn't nailed down.

Steve said the shrink was a "genius." Lola was precisely what the two of them needed during a complicated emotional period. Both fell madly in love with the dog, Melanie remembered, and their marriage found the focal point it needed.

There was no longer any confusion about how they'd spend much of their free time. Steve left his home-entertainment console to walk Lola together with Melanie, who worked at home. They went to a twice-weekly intensive obedience course at a training center in Madison, then an advanced class with the center's best trainer.

Their house and yard were now littered with balls, tug toys, and rawhide chews. On weekends they might drive to Sandy Hook, where Lola could run on the beach. So that the dog, who was energetic and highly social, could have some friends, they joined a play group for three dogs on their block.

"It was like she was a gift from up above," Melanie put in. "I know it sounds weird to say that, but she was just what we needed. We both adore her. She is so happy to see us when we come home. Believe me, we are not nutty people, but she gave us the glue we needed at that point."

It isn't, Steve hastened to point out, as if the dog had solved all their problems. They were still struggling to have a child, more than one if they could, and it was a fraught and draining process. (They were willing to adopt if necessary.) But their marriage was not in any doubt, and they no longer felt the need for counseling.

The role of dog as couple-saver, in fact, seems to be part of a trend. *American Demographics* magazine reported on the pet industry's scramble to keep up with the changing demographics of pet ownership in its May 2002 issue. Only a third of today's pet owners were married with children, according to Mediamark Research, Inc. There was, however, an increase in dog owner-ship among young couples who were living together before having children "as a means of testing the waters of parenthood," the article said.

At the other end of the demographic scale, Mediamark found, married baby boomers were also filling their recently emptied nests with dogs. So were singles, especially divorcees, widowers, and seniors.

"These shifts," the article concludes, "have helped create what experts say is one of the most prominent attitudinal drives of pet industy growth: the increasing anthropomorphism, or humaniza-tion, of pets by their owners."

★   ★   ★

If there is a dark side to the use of dogs as emotional surrogates, it is what sometimes happens when the need for them ends or eases—as with Rushmore, the German shepherd whose owner had died and whose new owner was about to remarry.

Carolyn called Rachel to say she'd decided to move back to Brooklyn, to be closer to her friends, and that her new apartment building wouldn't take dogs. Sharpton was headed for southern Virginia, where her sister, who knew and loved the dog, lived on eight acres and Sharpton could chase rabbits all day long. Carolyn wondered if anyone there would grasp the meaning of his name.

"It's going to hurt," said Carolyn matter-of-factly. "It's a good place for him to live, and who knows? Maybe I'll be back there in a year or two."

The club was atrophying.

Sally, who'd always floated on the edges of the group, did eventually take up with her fellow doctor, with the support and approval of the club. But her new partner was allergic to pet dander, so the already somewhat neglected Christie would have to go. Sally was as responsible as she could be, taking out ads in local papers, screening prospective adopters herself. She found a young couple with some experience in dog training who were dying for a poodle. Maybe this would turn out better for the dog.

Janice had met an executive and fellow runner at her daughter's school play, and her attendance at club gatherings had become more sporadic. Chester was a big loss to the Divorced Dogs Club in his capacity as male role model. But he was wild about Janice's new squeeze. In fact, Janice cracked the group up one night when she described her new beau as being disturbingly like Chester—"loving, reliable, trustworthy, and not terribly bright."

Sounded great, the other women all agreed.

"Chester goes hunting and swimming now," Janice said in wonder. "I sometimes think Al came on to me to get the dog."

The dwindling group had planned a farewell dinner for Carolyn, but she had to cancel at the last minute because of some real-estate closing problems in Brooklyn. Rachel wondered if maybe she just couldn't handle another round of goodbyes. Carolyn left Montclair in October, and no one in the group saw or heard from her or Sharpton again.

The club considered building its membership with an invitation to Danielle, a friend of Cynthia's who was about to file for divorce. "Let's bring in somebody who did the leaving," was Cynthia's pitch. They asked Danielle to come along on one of their group walks, sort of an audition. But in the end, they decided to stay as they were.

Everyone liked Danielle, but nobody could stand her schnauzer, who nipped Chester and tangled

154

with Aviva. The Divorced Dogs Club had had enough experience with discord, thank you. "If we were looking for a fight," Rachel said, "we could call one of our exes."

CHAPTER 6

A DUET

My dogs heard the sounds before I did—someone crooning a song, and a dog baying intermittently in response. As we rounded a wooded corner at a park near our house, we came upon them: a woman sitting on a wooden bench, serenading a rust-colored Welsh corgi with enormous eyes.

She was singing to the tune of "Rudolph the Red-Nosed Reindeer" and gazing at the dog, who was focused just as intently on her, head tilted. The lyrics were primitive, the story timeless:

> *Harry the Welsh corgi*
> *Had really big, big ears.*
> *They never did stop growing*
> *Throughout the years.*
> *All of the other corgis*
> *Laughed at him and even jeered.*
> *They would tell poor Harry,*
> *Hey, man, your ears are queer . . .*

And Harry, we supposed, was singing back,

offering a joyous howl every third or fourth line. The woman looked pale and weary. Her distended stomach and brunette wig suggested chemotherapy. But there was a big smile on her face. Her corgi did, in fact, have Dumbo-sized ears. They could have helicoptered him right into the sky if he could flap them fast enough.

The song—it unfolded over several stanzas as we eavesdropped discreetly from behind a stand of trees—told the tale of a hapless corgi ridiculed and rejected by his peers until Santa arrived to confer acceptance.

The power of this intimate scene was mesmerizing, and it was a bit embarrassing to have stumbled upon it. When my dogs charged forward to greet Harry with the usual sniffing, circling, and investigating, the woman looked a bit mortified.

"Was I imagining things," I said, mostly to break the ice, "or were you singing to your dog?"

She blushed as she introduced herself—Donna Dwight—and struggled a bit to get up off the bench. She struck me as being about sixty; later I learned that she was in her late forties. But her balance was off and she moved slowly, with great fatigue.

"I admit it," she said with a smile and a shrug. "I sing to Harry all the time. We sing to each other. It's silly, isn't it?"

She'd worked as an office manager for an insurance company north of Princeton for twenty-five years, but she was planning to retire soon, she told me as we walked the park paths slowly with our dogs. Yes, she was sick, and was working fewer hours than before. She'd undergone a series of debilitating surgeries and chemotherapy treatments for breast cancer; they'd left her swollen and, as she put it, "wrung out."

She lived alone now, in a nearby garden-apartment complex, her husband having left a year after her diagnosis. She was a throwback in this rapidly yuppifying town, an office worker being supplanted by the wealthier professionals pouring in from New York with their small kids.

She wanted to be careful about conveying the "wrong impression" about her husband. "He isn't a bad guy, just not a strong guy," she said. "In a way, it was just as well. We were having problems before all this, to be honest, so it wasn't only about my being sick. And I think I would have ended up worrying about him all the time."

She stopped, remembering. "I made a big decision," she said. "I decided that since I had always loved dogs—my mutt Millie died a few years ago, and I still miss her—I was going to go through this with a dog. I know how that must sound, but I knew the loyalty and love that a dog is capable of. . . ." She leaned over to toss Harry a homemade peanut butter cookie.

"So I went to a breeder I found on the Internet and got Harry when he was nine weeks old. He was definitely the runt of the litter, the odd one out. I fell in love with him from the minute I saw those big ears and big eyes." That was four years earlier. Donna, as she liked to say, was stubborn about staying alive.

Every time she mentioned his name, Harry's head swiveled and he came running over for a pat and a smooch. Certain dogs just exude unrelenting sweetness; Harry was one of them. He and Donna kept the sort of continuous eye contact that trainers prize. In fact, Donna rarely had to utter commands; Harry simply went where she went.

If a dog could have a sense of humor—legions of dog lovers swear that they do—Harry had one. It was hard not to smile just looking at him. His expression had a permanent twinkle, those big eyes radiating curiosity and affection. But he was no clown. Corgis are working dogs, and few worked harder than Harry.

Donna, it became apparent over subsequent weeks and months, was in need. As she'd started spending more time in hospitals and doctors' offices, many of her friends had drifted away. She understood. "It was too hard for them," she said. "Between the divorce and the cancer, I think I had the mark of Cain on me. People just don't know what to do. It hurt at first, then I accepted it, and I decided to make my stand with Harry—the two of us. I know he isn't a person, and I don't treat him like one, but I couldn't have made a better choice."

Harry wasn't about to drift away. He rarely even *looked* away.

She referred repeatedly to The Plan. She had a plan. Step one: retire. Step two: buy a small farmhouse in rural Pennsylvania. Step three: make arrangements for Harry's life after she's gone—with her remaining close friend, Joan, a part-time real estate agent who loved dogs. Step four: when it's time, die in her peaceful new home, with Harry at her bedside. With her pension, savings, and benefits, she'd have just enough to pull The Plan off. She didn't figure on being around more than a year or two, anyway. Some of her remaining money would be earmarked for Harry's lifelong care.

Donna's apartment—in one of those nondescript brick complexes with a faux-aristocratic name—was orderly and comfortable, but spare. She'd hung framed posters of dogs and birds on the walls and scattered plants around the rooms, but there wasn't a lot of furniture; the sofas and chairs were functional and inexpensive.

A pair of binoculars and a thick guide to the birds of the Northeast sat on a coffee table, coated with a thin layer of dust. The wooden birdhouse by the bedroom window was unoccupied, the bins empty of food. Lots of things that used to interest Donna had fallen by the wayside; she led a pared-down life these days.

Mornings, she and Harry went for a walk in Brookdale Park or in the woods behind the complex. Then she drove to work, whenever and for as long as she was able. Home for a light supper: a small salad, soup, and a sandwich for her, a can of Pedigree for Harry. She skipped dessert—she didn't have much appetite—but she kept freeze-dried liver treats for Harry. They were expensive, $4.99 a can, so he got two or three a night, parceled out between dinner and bedtime.

Then an after-dinner walk, the last of the night. The TV would go on, and while Donna watched, she tossed a hard rubber ball for Harry, who growlingly pursued it all over the apartment, racing from one room to another until he was worn out. By nine P.M., after taking an elaborate array of pills, she was in bed. Harry had a cedar bed of his own, but he preferred to sleep in Donna's, alongside her pillow.

The apartment had a fenced postage-stamp of a patio where she and Harry could sit and take the sun. Technically, the place didn't permit dogs, but if owners didn't flaunt their existence, and if the dogs stayed quiet and didn't bite and their messes were cleaned up, nobody bothered them. Like many dog owners, Donna was unfailingly con-scientious about carrying biodegradable cleanup bags around in her purple fanny pack; she didn't want to give anybody reason to ban dogs.

When she felt down or "teary," as she some-times put it, Harry yelped, squirmed, and looked generally ridiculous with those huge ears, winning a smile or even a laugh. He apparently had scant tolerance for moping or brooding; at the first sign, he was up nosing around, getting Donna moving or singing. Sometimes he just pressed against her for a long cuddle.

Although truckloads of books and studies address this issue, it's almost impossible to know much about dogs' emotional lives with any real certainty. We make assumptions, but the dogs can't point out where we might be wrong. We can only observe and guess at the origins and complexity of the sometimes profound attachments between dogs and people. Any of our theories—and there are many—seems as good and true as any other. The emotional bonds shared by people and their dogs remain private and powerful, often unhindered by contradiction or reality, free to grow and expand in ways outsiders can never fully grasp.

Donna certainly wasn't imagining her relationship with a loving and attentive creature. She saw something very real. Harry seemed to understand that he had a task to perform, and he took his work seriously. Whenever Donna reached down, Harry's head was under her hand. While she read, he dozed. When she breathed oddly or groaned in pain, he stayed by her side as if Velcroed.

He went along as she visited her various doctors, waiting eagerly in the car, staring at the last spot he'd seen her, squealing with joy when she returned, even as she struggled to deal with uncomfortable procedures, a growing list of drugs and insurance forms, and a dismaying stream of bad news.

She'd lost much of her hair, gained and then lost weight as the result of some of the medications and procedures, struggled to summon the energy to get through each day. Through this, Harry helped in every way he could; and at times, he was the only thing that did.

Donna's friend Joan came by regularly, and she worked hard to build a relationship with Harry, bringing treats and toys and making a big fuss over him. He was obviously fond of her, as he was of almost everyone he met, but he stayed focused on Donna. Did he know something was wrong? Impossible to say. But he couldn't have worked any harder at watching over her.

"He means the world to me," Donna told me one day in the park. "It's hard for even my closest friends to talk to me about this, and my husband just cracked. Harry is my heart, he makes me smile, keeps me company, gets me off my butt."

In scores of interviews, I was struck by how often people referred to their dog as their "heart." In certain contexts and situations, dogs are able to connect with the deepest part of a person, with someone's heart and soul, and that was what had happened here.

Donna was a strong, good-hearted, resourceful, and inherently optimistic person. She never complained about her illness or expressed bitterness

163

at the humans who fled when troubles beset her. She relied on a dog to ward off loneliness, provide activity and comfort.

But was this a good thing? Stories about dogs like Harry are always related with warmth and wonder, but I was sometimes haunted by the idea that Donna should have had more people caring for her, not just a devoted corgi. Harry couldn't talk to her about her illness or her death the way friends or relatives would.

In a different kind of society, or even this one fifty years ago, surely she would have been surrounded by her extended family, the members of a church, friends, neighbors, or perhaps a husband who wouldn't turn away.

But in the absence of such rootedness, in the absence of community, I hated to think of her without that big-eared corgi. He was doing a hell of a job.

"It's a simple relationship. What he does is make me feel loved, and what he also does is keep me concentrating on loving back," she explained one night. "I need that. I don't think dogs are a replacement for people. Yet sometimes they are, aren't they?"

Donna was slowing down, going to the park less frequently, making more excursions by car. She grew easily fatigued and felt the chill of the approaching winter. But she was a cheery e-mailer, sending me new songs she'd written for Harry, tales of their errands around town; recipes for dog treats she'd concocted, along with enthusiastic stories of their adventures.

"I just made Harry some carob balls from a recipe I got from the *Three Dog Bakery Cookbook*," she reported one day. "He ate three of them." The carob balls included skim milk, honey, vanilla, bran flakes, and carob powder. But his absolute favorite was Taffy's Camp Cookies (from a Vermont summer camp for people and their dogs called Camp Gone to the Dogs; Donna and Harry had been campers there a few summers ago).

When her friend Joan could drive them, Donna and Harry still took longer treks. They went to the Jersey shore to walk briefly on the beach on a windy Saturday morning and then stopped for some clam chowder. They went out to see the foliage near the Delaware Water Gap. And then: a surprise Donna had been scheming for Harry.

She decided Harry should do some sheepherding.

Donna had been thinking about this for a long time, e-mailing herders online, seeking advice from people with herding dogs. She knew she would be getting progressively weaker, and she thought of herding as a gift for Harry, the kind she might not be able to offer in the future. "He's a corgi, isn't he? He ought to see some sheep."

She and Joan went online and found a shepherd in upstate New York, and one bright day in late fall, she and Harry took the three-hour drive in Joan's Subaru wagon to rendezvous with some sheep.

Donna was as cheerful and good-humored as ever, though thinner, paler, weaker, sometimes even a bit disoriented. And she was always cold now, wearing scarves and sweatshirts and an extra layer of socks, even on mild, sunny days like this. Her bouts with nausea and diarrhea were more frequent, which made traveling more difficult. But she was nothing if not game.

I followed behind in my pickup with my two border collies, both of whom had already done some herding. Donna, mindful of my dogs as well as her Harry, had insisted they come. "We'll make it a party," she said. She'd brought three plastic containers filled with water, a shepherd's crook she'd found on the Net, a brimmed hat for the sun, enough treats and biscuits for a kennel, and a new herding song she'd written for Harry, to the tune of the Beatles' "Hey Jude."

> *Har-ry,*
> *You herding dog,*
> *They are fast sheep,*
> *But you will catch them.*
> *It's really a short but fast little trip,*
> *But when you get up there,*
> *You'll crack like a whip!*

Like the herding instructor and Joan, I was a bit nervous about this excursion. Herding can be intense, smelly, and unnerving, with sheep and dogs racing all over the place. Unlike some of the

166

people on the Discovery Channel, real herding-dog handlers have to move a *lot*—sometimes very quickly. Dogs could behave unpredictably around sheep; and, not uncommonly, the sheep returned the favor. The closest Harry had ever come to livestock was barking at some horses when they'd visited a farm in Bucks County.

Donna pooh-poohed such worries. She had complete confidence in her dog. "It's in Harry's blood," she kept saying. "Think of the fun he'll have."

Three hours later, we pulled into Columbia Farm, its lush green pastures highlighted by a red barn and a white frame farmhouse built before the Civil War.

Because of Donna's advance work, the farm's owner, Sarah Harding, had already set up a lawn chair outside a small pen. Inside were six mellow, "dog-broke" sheep, as Sarah whispered to Joan and me. What she meant was that these sheep were old and slow and had worked with dogs for years. They would anticipate the dog and move along without having to be chased, pushed, or bullied. Even a novice like Harry could handle them.

Sarah was thinking of Harry, she confided. Panicked sheep, who can run fast and weigh up to 300 pounds, will sometimes plow into dogs, as well as people. A small dog that didn't know how to respond could get hurt.

The sheep, distinctly unexcited, looked benign enough. They took in Harry, then continued nosing around for grass. After the long drive, Donna walked slowly, shielding her eyes from the glare. She was sweating one minute and shivering the next. Despite her bravura, she looked a little unsteady. But she was also determined and pulled out a visored cap, a scarf for her neck, and her tiny 35-mm camera. "I'm ready," she said, settling into the chair and aiming the camera.

Harry looked a bit anxious, keeping his eyes on Donna rather more than the sheep. He sat down alongside her.

Sarah explained the principles of herding to Donna and Joan—and to Harry, who listened raptly. He was relaxing, enjoying the company and the ubiquitous treats, though he had so far made no apparent connection between himself and the grazing sheep.

"Okay," asked Sarah. "We ready?"

Donna nodded, and Sarah put Harry on a leash—he hesitated, looking doubtful—and gently led him toward the pen, unlatched the gate, and walked him in. The sheep, understanding their role, moved toward the far corner.

Harry, stressed, looked back toward Donna, then at Sarah, then at the sheep. His big eyes widened even further, and his enormous ears shot back. Donna was shouting encouragement from the sidelines: "Go, Harry, you can get 'em. Go herd those sheep!"

Sarah took him off the lead. Her own border collie, Blaze, lay crouched outside the pen, available for backup. But as the sheep shuffled around a bit, Harry trotted briskly back the way he'd come, his ears flattened, and he pushed with his nose at the gate to get out. Sarah let him out and he rushed back to Donna and ducked behind her chair, peering out at the sheep.

"It's okay, boy, don't worry about it," she said soothingly, tossing him some bits of thawed meatball. He kept peering up at her, then back at the sheep. She looked concerned—for Harry.

Sarah had an idea. "Donna, would you be comfortable just stepping inside the pen, near the gate? I'll stand in front of you and bring Blaze in. That might help Harry feel more comfortable." Donna cast a what-on-earth-am-I-doing look at Joan, then walked stiffly into the pen with Harry. Sarah and Blaze took up protective positions a foot or two in front of Donna, who tossed Harry a bit of meatball, along with words of encouragement. "It's okay, Harry. Go for it."

Twice Harry ventured out toward the big woolly animals and retreated to safety behind Donna; then he steeled himself to approach the sheep again. They lifted their heads and looked at him evenly, then resumed their crunching—until Blaze, without even bothering to move, grew impatient and gave an authoritative bark. Then the sheep backed up, though slowly, five or six feet into the corner of the pen. Harry advanced confidently, and barked also. The sheep moved a few feet more, for the most part out of politeness. The audience exploded.

"Yay!" Joan and Donna were applauding and whooping as Harry preened, beamed, and walked slowly back toward the gate. Sarah opened it and he came strutting out with Donna, the triumphant herder and dog. Donna was exultant, shrieking with praise and excitement and showering him with treats. The sheep looked both relieved and puzzled, and returned to their grazing.

"What a brave boy you are!" Donna said.

Sarah was clapping, too. "He's really got it," she said. "That's some herding boy, some working dog."

They chatted for a bit and then Donna, who had managed to snap nearly a full roll of photos of the brief encounter—soon to appear all over her apartment—said her goodbyes and walked slowly back toward the car. She and Joan got in; Harry hopped into the back, poking his head out the window for a final proud review of the sheep before they headed off for lunch and then home to New Jersey.

"I told you doubters," said Donna. "He's got the genes!"

A month or two later, Donna called to say she would love some company. She and her apartment were radically transformed: she'd grown still paler, her head was swathed in a scarf, and the apartment was littered with medical equipment—a portable

170

IV, a wheelchair, an oxygen mask, bottles of pills. Twice a day, home health-care aides came by to wash the dishes, change the sheets, take Donna's blood pressure, and check on her growing list of medications.

For perhaps the first time, the pain she must have been feeling all along was evident in her face. If she had looked sixty when I first saw her, she looked even older now. She had ups as well as downs, she said, but at the moment, she was down. It could go on that way for some time.

There was no more talk of moving out to the country, to her and Harry's dream house. "I think my timing was off on that," she observed philosophically. She'd hired a dog walker to take Harry out during the day, and Joan came by in the evening when she could. Sometimes Donna just let Harry outside. He knew what to do, and did it quickly.

Harry himself seemed a bit grayer, more serious and anxious, but he was working just as hard.

"What a guy!" Donna exclaimed. "Thank God for him." Sometimes, she said, she would vomit before she could make it to the bathroom. Once in a while she'd fall. Other times she'd drift into a drowsy, medicated sleep. But wherever she was, whatever was happening, Harry was always right there with her.

Almost always. At Donna's insistence, the corgi was spending one or two afternoons a week with Joan. But he seemed to be doing something that behaviorists insist dogs cannot do: reading a complex human situation.

At Joan's—though she hadn't told Donna this—Harry wouldn't eat or sit still. He paced, whined, rushed to the door and sat there fixedly. When Joan finally relented, he dashed to her car and peered eagerly out the window until they returned to Donna's apartment.

"I have no doubt that once this is all over, he and I will do fine. But this is a dog with a mission," Joan said soberly. "Nothing will stop him—not food, treats, or anything I can do."

It seemed to be the case. Harry's eyes fastened on Donna like a laser beam. He moved from room to room with her, hopped up onto the bed and dozed with her when she slept, accompanied her to the bathroom, stood by while she threw up. It was not an easy scene, for humans or dogs, but Harry clearly had no desire to be anywhere else. He might not have wanted to push sheep around, but he was ready to work with Donna.

Even sometimes in her sleep, she'd reach over and Harry would be right there, ready to accept a scratch or offer a lick. He never seemed to get in her way, trip her up, or tangle the cables and tubes that had sprouted in her apartment.

On this visit, she unveiled her latest song, written to the tune of "Jingle Bell Rock."

Harry Dwight, Harry Dwight, Ha-aaaaary Dwight,

Harry Dwight's mine and things'll be fine.
Harry came to me from far, far away,
And he's here to stay . . .

"It may need some tweaking," she offered in a soft, raspy voice. Harry didn't seem to think so. As he always did when she sang to him, he yelped along, wagged his stump of a tail, and covered her face with kisses.

CHAPTER 7

A KID AND HIS DOG

For his fourteenth birthday, Jamal Sutton asked his mother for a dog. He became obsessed with the idea. He loved dogs, he told his mother, and had wanted one ever since his father moved out three years earlier and took a job in Virginia.

Jamal was tall and shy and mild-mannered. He had been a bookish kid, before he realized the stigma that went along with that. Now he'd developed the protective coloration that helped him blend in. Like every other kid on the block, he worshiped Michael Jordan and, lately, Shaquille O'Neal and Kobe Bryant of the L.A. Lakers. He listened to hip-hop—Outkast, Snoop Dogg, Jay-Z, Ludacris—day and night, on the way to school, during many of his classes, on his way home, and while hanging out in Nishuane Park, at the opposite end of town from Mills Reservation. Still, he remained something of a loner, with few close friends since his buddy Malik had moved away.

Though he wasn't especially muscular, Jamal hoped to develop as an athlete. "I'm fast rather

174

than strong," was the way he put it. He played basketball for Montclair High's junior varsity, though he didn't get a lot of playing time, and earned decent if not spectacular grades.

Several of his teachers liked him, fussed over him, bugged him to work harder, to get on the college-prep track—he was a freshman—and realize his considerable potential. But he wasn't buying it. Such attention only brought derision from buddies, who accused him of sucking up, and made his social life worse. He didn't expect to go to college, he said, unless he got a basketball scholarship.

Jamal's yearning for a dog, his mother knew, had a lot to do with wanting status in the neighborhood, protection from a cluster of kids who had been taunting and bullying him.

At first, after she assented, he visited several shelters in search of a pit bull or rottweiler, the breeds he favored. He tried Montclair, neighboring Bloomfield, even, after a long bus trek, Newark. At each place, the staff all advised him to come back with a grown-up.

Then a friend down the block told him about a post-office worker whose pit bull bitch had recently given birth to a litter. The "breeder" was charging twenty-five dollars for a puppy. Jamal worked at various after-school jobs whenever he wanted money for clothes, CDs, or candy; he stocked shelves at a variety store, shopped for Mrs. Edwards down the block, cleaned up in front of St. Paul's Baptist Church. He could come up with twenty-five dollars. So he picked a speckled, black-and-brown puppy, the biggest and most energetic one, and named him Dre.

Jamal lived in southeastern Montclair, where it bordered East Orange. By urban standards, it wasn't a particularly rough neighborhood. By Montclair's, it was the poorest, most crime-beset corner of town.

His family rented the ground floor of a ninety-year-old woodframe duplex. Six people lived there: his mother, a supervisor for New Jersey Transit in Newark; his grandmother; two sisters, one of whom Jamal shared a room with; and a stepsister.

The gardens and lawn of the brown-and-white house were lovingly tended; the house itself was not. The Suttons' plumbing broke down regularly, the window screens were torn, the wiring was constantly shorting out, and the paint had peeled inside and out. The adjacent two-family houses, some in similar disrepair, stood close enough that their occupants could overhear their neighbors' conversations and smell one another's dinners cooking.

The streets looked dirtier than most Montclair streets on this crisp early autumn day, scattered with windblown debris. Jamal and his mother, Alishia, both said there was a drug problem on the street. Part of life these days, Alishia said.

★   ★   ★

Unlike many Montclair kids, Jamal wasn't picking out a puppy from a breeder's website or finding a furry gift under his Christmas tree. His gift was his mother's permission. If he wanted a dog, he had to find one.

Like most Montclair dog owners, however, Jamal was crazy about his pet, even though he treated him differently than most. Dre was chained to a fencepost all day while Jamal was in school.

Dre had the classic pit bull look—massive, at about seventy-five pounds, with bright, curious eyes, a big barrel chest, and that famous square head held high. Like most, Dre was instinctively friendly around people, although protective of his home and wary of strangers, and he was attached to Jamal in particular.

When Jamal walked home from school, the first thing he did was go to the yard and call the dog—"Yo, Dre!"—who barked, jumped up to lick him, and wagged his tail in frenzied greeting. The yard was tiny, hemmed in by the houses behind it and on either side, and paved with concrete, except for a skinny tree in the middle. It smelled of dog waste.

The second thing Jamal did was pick up a thin wooden board. The dog's demeanor changed as soon as he saw the board; he stiffened, then retreated, growling softly. He showed all the signs of canine stress: cowering, turning his head away, laying his ears back, squinting, panting. Once or twice he showed some teeth, but only briefly, and Jamal seemed not to notice or care. Dre looked frantically around for a way out, but there was none: the yard was surrounded by a chain-link fence.

So he stopped looking for an escape and turned to face his owner. Jamal slammed him in the side of the head with the board. The dog yelped and jumped back. Then he hit him in the side and rump and poked at his back and shoulder. Expressionless, businesslike, Jamal poked and hit him again and again. He didn't strike hard enough to draw blood. But he beat Dre sharply—though not brutally, if one can make such a distinction—on and off, for about ten minutes. It was difficult to watch.

The dog became increasingly aroused, then angry, snarling and growling. In a few minutes, he was nearly out of control, barking, lunging at Jamal, snapping back. He'd gone from welcoming to frightening.

When Jamal felt Dre was ready, he stopped, waited five minutes, then threw Dre some crackers and filled his water bowl. The agitated, panting dog gulped half of it down. Then Jamal tied a rope around his neck and took him into the house, yelling at his youngest sister to stay away. Dre had stopped growling and barking but still showed the signs of arousal: stiff posture, tail up, his head moving back and forth. Jamal shouted to his grandmother that he and Dre were going out for a walk.

There were quite a few people on the street—sitting on stoops, pushing babies in strollers, playing ball, walking dogs, coming home from school. A woman walking a small mutt came within ten feet, then noticed Dre and pulled her dog back from the sidewalk. A mother pushing an infant moved abruptly into the street. The kids playing ball stopped and retreated to their stoops until Jamal and Dre passed.

"He's never hurt anybody, I don't see him ever doing that," Jamal said as he walked Dre ahead of him. "But I don't want him walking around being sweet and friendly to everybody. He's supposed to look tough. People respect him and they respect me."

They were headed for Nishuane Park, a few blocks away, where he sometimes played basketball—or had, his mother told me, until a new gang of kids claimed the court.

The neighborhood was, in some ways, more connected to Newark and the Oranges than to the rest of Montclair. Once in a great while, Jamal said, he'd bike up into the wealthier sections to swim at a town pool or just to ride around, but he had no friends there and few reasons to go. His mother had only been to Upper Montclair once that she could recall, to see a movie at the Bellevue Cinema with a friend and eat at a nearby Japanese restaurant.

Their lives centered mostly on the southern part of town. They shopped at the stores along Bloomfield Avenue, the township's main business district, and bought groceries at the nearby Pathmark, where prices were lower. Their church—Alishia insisted that Jamal and his sisters go to St. Paul's every Sunday morning—was in the South End too.

Since they had so little contact with the town outside their schools and neighborhoods, both Jamal and his mother assumed that in most ways life hereabouts wasn't radically different than in the rest of Montclair, though even the rumor of a drug dealer on the streets of Upper Montclair would probably have touched off a parental riot.

The park, a green oasis, came into view.

Jamal shrugged off questions about getting pushed around in school, though he admitted he'd been chased out of the park more than once by a bunch of kids who biked over from East Orange, two of whom went to Montclair High. (For years, kids from adjoining towns have registered in the vaunted Montclair schools, using the addresses of friends or relatives living in town; some get rooted out and have to transfer, while others are never caught.)

Jamal was usually monosyllabic in his responses, both wary and shy. When especially sensitive questions arose, he wouldn't utter even a syllable. He didn't want to offer any details about this turf struggle, for example, or provide any names.

As they neared the park entrance, Dre picked up on the idea that they were going to work. This, after all, was his mission, what Jamal wanted of him.

The other kids hanging around couldn't take their eyes off the dog, and Dre returned the favor, locking onto them with a focused intensity that was unnerving, almost daring somebody to start something. Nobody did. Jamal, eyes fixed straight ahead, walked right alongside the basketball court, and nobody said a word.

Four guys, all wearing various pro sports paraphernalia—a Knicks jersey, a Lakers cap, a Raiders shirt—were shooting hoops; two more kids stood by the fence, laughing, ragging on the players, waiting their turn. On the nearby playground, smaller children were chasing around, bouncing balls, riding the swings.

The kids by the court, watching Jamal, said something to the others and everyone laughed. One phrase—"little bitch"—filtered through. Jamal turned toward the group with Dre, and everybody grew quiet, suddenly absorbed in basketball. He strolled right across the center of the court. The four players backed up and looked away. A low rumble came from Dre, perhaps picking up on Jamal's tension. Jamal, offering a rare smile, walked on; he said Dre was doing a good job.

A local vet had given me Jamal's name after I'd spoken to her about the ways dogs worked these days and the ways people interacted with them. She'd seen Dre only once, after he was hit by a car and suffered a broken leg. Jamal was supposed to bring him back to have the cast removed and the leg X-rayed, but she never saw him again. She suspected it was an economic issue.

It was not uncommon, she told me, for people to beat their dogs to arouse them for security work or personal protection. Many of the dogs she saw were banged up much worse than Dre, who was healthy, she recalled, and generally well cared for.

"If it's really bad, I call the shelter or the police," the vet told me. "But I didn't feel comfortable doing that in this case. The kid and the dog loved each other, for one thing. Besides, if the shelter took him, it would probably be a death sentence."

Dog behaviorists generally agree that breeds like pit bulls, rottweilers, and German shepherds can make fine pets. Most are not naturally aggressive; that's a taught, not innate, behavior. But that is little comfort to parents or others who might come into contact with them. When something goes wrong, the consequences can be severe, and something goes wrong often enough that fear of these dogs has become epidemic, even though Humane Society statistics show that Labradors bite many more people than pit bulls. Lawsuits involving such dogs are skyrocketing, and some insurers no longer approve policies for homes where pit bulls live.

It was the postal worker who sold Dre to Jamal who'd taught him how to "crank up the dog." That guy really beat his dogs, Jamal said. He drew blood, left scars.

By poking, hitting, and provoking Dre, Jamal was arousing a dog with powerful hunting and fighting instincts. Oddly, though, Jamal was also unconsciously skilled at calming Dre down. The result was that the dog did both things well.

When they got home, the two holed up in Jamal's bedroom for hours, listening to hip-hop. Jamal talked quietly to the dog, offered Dre bits of bread, sometimes dog biscuits from the grocery store. The food and the attention was calming, the attachment strong; after a few minutes, Dre was like a lap dog, licking Jamal.

The dog ventured into other parts of the house briefly, but always returned to Jamal, who responded with affection, scratching Dre's stomach, playing tug-of-war with a knotted-up old towel. Sometimes Dre won.

Safe in his room, which held twin beds for him and his youngest sister, Ashama, Jamal still read a lot, mostly comic books and sports magazines and mysteries. There was a computer for the kids to share, but because of the wiring problems it kept blowing out and sat unused on a desk.

Once or twice Jamal took up a sci-fi tale, borrowed from the school library or given him by a pesky English teacher who kept prodding him to think about college. Dre liked to curl up alongside him as he read.

"Abuse" is among the most frequently uttered words in the dog world these days. Plenty of Montclair owners walked around with dogs they believed had formerly been abused. This one *was* abused, every day, yet he also loved and was loved by his shy, needy, and isolated owner.

Jamal simply shrugged whenever the question of the beatings—which were, of course, illegal—came up. "I just hit him to juice him up, to get him ready to go out." Dre walked with a slight limp now, but Jamal thought that was cool, like a battle scar. Although Dre had never harmed a person, Jamal conceded that he'd had a few ugly run-ins with some neighborhood dogs.

So silent and impassive much of the time, Jamal grew more animated whenever he talked about "my man Dre." His love for the dog was beyond question. He was with Dre almost every second he was home, taking him for several more walks before bedtime. Dre slept at the foot of Jamal's bed.

His exchanges with his family were brief and to the point—"Yo, Sham, what's for dinner?" But he communicated a fair amount with Dre, reciting rap lyrics to the dog in the relative privacy of his room. It was not lost on Alishia that her son talked to the dog more than to any human.

No one else in the household had much to do with Dre. Jamal's Grandma Alma was standoffish, disapproving of his treatment, even though the dog seemed especially fond of her. She told Jamal so, repeatedly. "It's not right to beat on that dog. He loves you!" she'd yell from her seat in the living room, where she was watching TV. "I know, Grandma," Jamal would say soothingly, respectfully.

Of the three sisters, only Ashama spent a little time with Dre. The others avoided him, and their mother was usually at work.

Alishia worried about Jamal, in the particular way that harried single mothers, without a partner to talk to or strategize with, worry about headstrong sons. He had his father's temper, she said, and had gotten into a few fights in recent months.

His family situation was even more compli- cated than he knew. Alishia—a tall, soft-spoken woman of forty-two with simple, straight hair and no jewelry except a wedding ring—told me that Jamal's father, an army computer programmer, had actually left before he was born. She thought Jamal had half-guessed at the truth, but he never asked about it. She would make sure he understood the whole story by the time he graduated from high school, she said.

The "father" he'd grown up with "told me he wanted to have a family, but he didn't," she said. "He was raised rough, and so Jamal was treated rough sometimes. It never got too bad, but it got bad. One of the reasons he moved on out of here." She thought having men he loved leave him was one reason Jamal didn't always trust people.

I couldn't help thinking of Jamal's own treat- ment of Dre—not too bad, but bad. Or of the dog's unswerving loyalty and protection.

Alishia was right: Jamal didn't trust many people.

He never spoke of his father or answered questions about him. His response was always the same: a shrug. He did say it was hard sometimes, living in a house full of women.

Like many single mothers, Alishia worked under intense pressure, juggling a million details at once, always looking over her shoulder to check on her kids and her mother. She took pride in her job, helping to man the control room of New Jersey Transit's vast operations center in Newark. But she worked a different shift each week and, given her civil servant's salary of $34,000 and the six people she was supporting, she was happy to accept any overtime that came her way. So she often worked six days a week, as many as twelve hours a day.

She checked on each of her kids daily, either in person or by phone, to make sure they were where they were supposed to be, properly dressed, doing their homework for school or Sunday school, saying their prayers before bed.

Despite her grueling schedule, the house was clean and neat, though sparsely furnished and sometimes noisy from the TV in the living room and Jamal's hip-hop and Dre's barking at passersby.

Watchful and respected, she insisted that the kids help with household chores and pick up their own messes: dirty clothes went to the overflowing laundry hamper in the center hallway, and the kids took turns vacuuming the apartment and keeping an eye on their grandmother. Jamal also took out the garbage, washed the dishes a few times a week, and picked up food at the supermarket when his mom left him a list. And, of course, he took care of Dre. This was a lot of household responsibility, especially compared with the average Montclair teenager.

"Jamal is a good boy," Alishia told me one evening after work. She was shy, like her son, and constantly fatigued, but proud of her family. "He behaves very well. It's those girls I'm really worried about.

"When he said he wanted a dog, as a pet and for some protection, I could understand that, it made sense to me. He really wanted a dad after Joe left, and I felt guilty about that. So after two or three years of him bothering me, I said okay. Because there *are* some problems in the neighborhood, and he convinced me that a dog could protect him, the house, and his sisters." A lot of kids had big dogs, she said. It gave them some standing.

She had little to do with Dre, or the way in which Jamal cared for him. She had never been around dogs much and was afraid of them, of pit bulls in particular. Dre had never harmed or menaced any of the family—she wouldn't have put up with that. But, otherwise, "It's Jamal's dog. He takes care of him. He doesn't mess with me."

The decision to get a dog is often more complicated than it seems.

Veterinarians estimate the lifetime cost of owning an eighty-pound dog at $8,353, a ten-pound dog at $3,525, and a cat at $3,957. These figures—cited by Alexa Albert and Kris Bulcroft in *Journal of Marriage and the Family* several years ago—are for city pets and include licensing, grooming, veterinary costs, and occasional boarding. (Americans spend $5 billion a year feeding dogs and cats alone, the researchers reported, and only $3 billion on baby food.)

"Pets do not make economic sense, particularly in the city," the researchers concluded. True, some dogs were used in therapy, guided the blind, or provided protection. "But beyond these small fractions, pets do not do useful work, and they provide no profit despite the fact that they cost substantial amounts of money, require time, and often exact humiliating or onerous tasks from their owners."

In short, said Albert and Bulcroft, pets are an economic liability, particularly when contrasted with the other needs of a modern, urban household. It was precisely that paradox that raised some of the more fascinating questions about dogs' roles in modern families.

Of course, Jamal saw no paradox; he wouldn't agree that dogs perform no useful functions. Although he wasn't especially articulate about it and found his need for a dog even tougher to talk about than did Rob Cochran, who lived a couple of miles up Grove Street, he

188

maintained that "My life is better and safer and more fun with this dog—*that* I can tell you."

In families with emotional turbulence, divorced or single-parent families, the attachment of kids to dogs can become even stronger.

According to a 2001 study by two Australian psychologists in the journal *Anthrozoos*, the intensity of young children's feelings toward dogs was significantly higher in single-parent families, and for obvious reasons: a dog could provide children with emotional support in families that offered limited access to "significant other humans."

Dr. Peter Fonagy, one of the architects of attachment theory, has written that a child with early attachment issues can be prone to moodiness, poor verbal skills, poor peer relations, and symptoms of depression and aggression, right up to and through preadolescence.

Why wouldn't Jamal have such issues? The father he knew had left abruptly; Jamal had only seen him once in the past three years. He took no active interest in his son's life and, Alishia lamented, provided no financial support. Even when he had been around, he'd had little to do with Jamal and was, she said, "moody, nasty, and unpredictable."

In fact, the year Jamal was born was one of the toughest in her life; he was actually raised mostly by her mother until he was two, when Alishia started taking community college classes and "got my life together, with the Lord's help."

Alishia knew about Jamal's daily beating of the dog—her mother had told her—and had advised Jamal she thought it was wrong. "But I understand it," she said.

"He wants to walk down that street with his head high, with a dog that's strong and puffed up, and I have to tell you, as his mother, I want the same thing. He sure feels safer since Dre. And it's his business.

"I don't know anything about dogs, but I can tell you this—those two love each other. I wouldn't want to be the person that got in between them."

CHAPTER 8

A TALE OF TWO DOGS

Like so many Montclair kids, Keith O'Brien woke up early Christmas morning. His parents had been hinting for weeks that he was getting something special, something he'd treasure, something he'd "never forget." He couldn't remember their ever being so excited about a present.

Until recently, he would have guessed that the gift was Microsoft's new Xbox console, which Keith, a passionate gamer, coveted more than anything.

But his father had brought the Xbox home for his birthday a few weeks earlier. Perhaps he was getting a new computer, something his parents had told him was a year or two away. He knew they'd brought something into the basement early on Christmas Eve. Maybe they were just trying to fool him.

It was eight A.M. when he ran downstairs and there, jumping around excitedly in a plastic crate, was a twelve-week-old yellow Lab puppy, the most appealing thing he'd seen in his ten years.

His eight-year-old sister, Katrina, went tearing downstairs at the same time but stopped when she noticed the tag affixed to the crate: MERRY CHRISTMAS, KEITH. HERE'S RUDY.

"It's Keith's dog, but it's for the whole family," their mother said when she and their father came downstairs in their bath-robes. "It's a family dog." Katrina got a hamster.

Rudy was a great-looking pup, the kind seen romping in magazine ads and on TV commercials, with nearly white fur, melting dark eyes, and floppy ears.

Nobody could help cooing over adorable Rudy, but he could certainly be a pest sometimes. In his first few days with the O'Briens, he chewed rugs and shoes and jumped up on people. He could be fun: Keith and the dog liked to wrestle and play tug-of-war. They were an adorable sight, the blond boy and the blond dog, tussling on the carpet. Problem was, Rudy liked to play a bit *too* much. He'd often grab somebody's pant leg or sweatshirt sleeve, growling exuberantly, and rip it as often as not.

But if Keith liked playing with the dog, he wasn't wild about walking or feeding him. This was an old story with kids and dogs, the subject of considerable parental eye-rolling: the reality of what happens after the puppy comes home. The senior O'Briens were a bit disappointed at Keith's reaction. At first, he rushed home from school to play with Rudy. A week or two later, he barely seemed to notice that Rudy was around.

This wasn't really Keith's fault. He'd never actually asked for a puppy or volunteered to take on dog chores. He was usually at a crucial point in a computer game, already in his pajamas, or deep in a critical homework project when Rudy needed his evening walk. Sometimes, when it was rainy or cold outside, his parents didn't feel they should even ask him.

The O'Briens didn't know or think all that much about dogs. Busy with demanding careers—Sam was an accountant with a big Manhattan firm, Gina an editor at a publishing conglomerate—they faced workdays that often stretched from eight A.M. to eight P.M. Their nanny, Carmen, filled in the gaps. That left precious little time for dog training.

When they thought about Rudy at all, they fell back on conventional wisdom or intuition. Gina thought dog crates seemed cruel and refused to use one. Sam believed in the widely preached theory that dogs were pack animals who needed to be quickly and forcefully shown their place. He remembered his own father whaling the daylights out of their mutt—"a great dog"—when it misbehaved.

"I had dogs when I was a kid," he said, "and you have to let them know who's in charge. You have to let them have it, at least once, and then they get it."

193

So, during Rudy's first few weeks with the family, Sam let him have it—more than once. He whacked him on the butt or smacked him with a rolled-up newspaper, accompanied by bellowed reprimands, when Rudy made mistakes; and, naturally, he made plenty. Normal puppy behavior can be pretty revolting. Dogs, in essence, have to be trained to behave abnormally in order to live peaceably with humans in houses. Humans want love, support, and good manners, not all of which are on a dog's instinctive agenda.

The puppy looked abashed, even frightened when he got whacked or yelled at. But in the resilient way of Labs, he recovered his high spirits quickly. Contrary to Sam's ideas, Rudy didn't seem to have gotten it.

In the house directly across the street, Diane Winship was sitting on the floor in joyous communion with *her* new puppy on Christmas morning, a sleek black Belgian sheepdog she'd already named Chaos. Diane was thirty years older than Keith, but they were doing essentially the same thing—rolling on the floor with their dogs, getting their noses licked, scratching their dogs' tummies.

Unlike Keith, Diane was expecting this gift; in fact, she had badly wanted a dog. Her husband, Phil, didn't want to give her one she hadn't chosen herself, so after months of Web browsing, reading, and phone calls, he presented her with the name of a breeder in Michigan. He was certain he'd found one of the best Belgian breeders in the country, especially after the guy grilled Phil endlessly about their lives, kids, home, yard, and attitudes toward canines. He even had a breeder friend from Ramsey drive over to check the Winships out.

The dog was shipped directly from Detroit to Newark, and Phil, an economist at J.P. Morgan, went to the airport to pick him up. Like his neighbors, he planned to keep the dog in the basement until Christmas morning. But Diane didn't last an hour. She and the kids, a seven-year-old and a ten-year-old, crept into the basement the night before and it was love at first sight all around.

Chaos was jet black and beautiful, small enough to hold in their arms (though in a few months he'd weigh nearly as much as the younger child), affectionate and slurpy. Bright and intensely curious, he seemed to notice everyone and everything, from noises outside to the voices wafting from the upstairs TV.

Having done their homework, the Winships had small crates ready: in the kitchen; by the back door; up in the bedroom where they all knew Chaos would eventually sleep. They'd scattered squeaky toys, balls, and rawhide chews (the hard, twisted kind that vets approve of because puppies can't choke on them) around the house to keep him busy and prevent his gnawing on other, less expendable things.

Diane had already been on the phone interviewing trainers and had found one she liked who would come to the house an hour a week. It was expensive—$500 over two months—but she thought one-on-one training in familiar surroundings would be more effective than a class. Besides, the trainer said he'd also be available for follow-up advice for the duration of the dog's life. Diane's diligence was a rarity in Montclair, where people regularly shelled out small fortunes on lessons for their kids but frequently thought dog training a silly waste of money.

Diane, though, had it all plotted out. Chaos would stay in the kitchen until he was housebroken, which was simpler when owners were willing to use crates. That way she could avoid shouting, scolding, swatting, or pushing the dog's nose in its own waste.

"I was very careful and deliberate about it," Diane recalled of this getting-acquainted period. "I've seen how many untrained dogs there are. I hate the way people are always screaming at them. I wanted my relationship with Chaos to be great from the first, to be one of trust and love."

She was one of the handful of Montclair people I'd met who had given training this much thought. She'd ordered several books, ranging in approach from the traditional (dogs are pack animals who need to learn their places) to the positive (dogs are trained by reinforcing the proper behavior, not by criticizing, calling attention to, or correcting the bad).

She decided she could pick and choose. Although

drawn instinctively to positive techniques, she wasn't reluctant to correct Chaos sharply—with a firm "no" or, more rarely, "bad"—if there were critical safety issues involved, like going into the street or chasing trucks. She'd learned from her research that in their desire to please their dogs, people often overstimulated them with too many toys, too frequent walks, too much wrestling, chewing, and tugging. Many dogs knew how to get excited, she realized, but few knew how to be calm.

The trainer didn't want to start work for a couple of weeks, until Chaos was four months old, but he was in agreement with her general philosophy. Meanwhile, he advised, the Winships should avoid too many "mouthing" games in which the dog was encouraged to bite, tug, or chew; they should remember to praise him when he was still, to get him used to being touched and stroked.

He was virtually housebroken in a week. "I only raised my voice to him once or twice," Diane said proudly. She was building the relationship she wanted, working at it.

For example, after some initial whining, Chaos willingly went into his chewbone-stocked crate. Diane made it a point to leave him there for fifteen, then thirty minutes a day, then an hour, so that he could reliably stay alone when the family went out. The crate—she'd read lots of warnings about this—was never to be used to punish; it was simply a private preserve, always well supplied with things to gnaw or eat.

"I'm no hard-ass, but I wanted to own the dog, I didn't want the dog to own me," she'd decided. "I wanted to be able to go out without feeling guilty, and without worrying that Chaos would eat the house up. I didn't want to be coming home with all of us tense about what we would find. Something in a book I read resonated with me: Don't give a dog a chance to get into trouble and he won't learn how."

Like most Labs, Rudy was enthusiastic, energetic, chewy, and messy, something Gina and Sam hadn't quite realized. When Rudy peed on the living room carpet, they both freaked. Sam grabbed him by the scruff of the neck, yelled, "No! Bad dog!" and then dragged him outside.

When he chewed through a laundry basket, Sam grabbed a half-eaten sweatshirt, pressed Rudy's face into it, and swatted him with *The New York Times Sunday Magazine*. The dog yelped, then cowered.

Once or twice Sam caught Rudy in the act of defecating; his response was to press the dog's nose into the feces and drag him into the yard—a fairly common housebreaking technique.

He also filled an empty soda can with a handful of coins—somebody at work had suggested this—and taped the top closed. When he saw the dog squatting or chewing, he'd throw the can on the floor, the clatter causing Rudy to yelp and run. A genial guy and loving husband and father, Sam considered none of these training techniques cruel or abusive. They were simply what he'd seen his father do. But as January turned into February, they weren't proving very effective.

Absent from the process, moreover, was the boy whose dog this supposedly was. Sam didn't like the way things were going. "We got the dog for Keith, but the truth is—and I know this isn't a new story—he loved the puppy, but he's not so interested in the dog the puppy is becoming. We all saw that cute face and didn't really picture the behemoth he's going to be. We're a bit over our heads." Sam had to admit it: "Keith just loves his friends and his computer games more."

He blamed himself, Sam added ruefully. He and Gina had never really discussed dog care with Keith.

"There was no void in Keith's life," Gina agreed. He was popular and busy, engaged in all sorts of things, from video games to real-life soccer. He rode his dirt bike all over the neighborhood and was learning the guitar. "We just made some assumptions."

One was that a kid's life wasn't complete without a dog, not an unusual impulse hereabouts. But unlike most of the things people think their kids should have—bikes, music lessons, summer camps—this one required devoted daily care, year after year. Kids are very likely to say they want a dog, and at the time they probably do. But their lives evolve rapidly and continuously, and what they want or need at any given point is fluid, at best.

Now Keith didn't feel compelled to take much responsibility for Rudy, and his parents didn't feel entitled to push him. Even if they did, he didn't know a lot about training a dog. Nor was he even home all that much.

Since Katrina couldn't handle the dog at all, and Carmen was wary of dogs in general, Rudy stayed cooped up in the pantry much of the day. He was thoroughly cranked by the time Carmen let him out into the backyard—though she didn't leave him out long, because he barked and dug holes in the lawn.

Soon the pantry couldn't hold him, either. With little to do, and not much exercise, he chewed his way through the cardboard barriers the O'Briens kept setting up before they left for work and school, pushed aside the chairs meant to prop up the cardboard, and vaulted easily over a kiddie gate that would've thwarted a toddler.

Even when the kids and Carmen were at home, the elder O'Briens often returned to find things destroyed—mail, table legs, sneakers—leading to more shouts and more newspaper-swatting. By now, Rudy wasn't much fun to be around. He jumped, lunged, barked, and slobbered, and nobody knew the commands that would make him stop.

Something significant had happened, although nobody quite realized it at the time. Emotionally, Rudy had been abandoned. He wasn't dumped in a park or taken to a shelter, but he had nevertheless become nobody's dog.

Though Labs are a patient, loving, and reliable breed, people sometimes forget that they were bred to hunt and work. They're big and strong and their instincts lead them to root around for food. They need training, but the O'Briens simply didn't have the time or will for it. Yet, curiously, they considered it unthinkable to give the dog away.

"Give Rudy up? No way. He's Keith's dog," was all Sam would say. I had the sense that he'd be embarrassed, too; the O'Briens were the kind of people who went to a shelter to *get* a dog, not drop one off.

"The dog is a constant pain in the ass," Sam acknowledged as winter waned. "We thought we were doing something great for our son, but now we can't quite remember why we did it." But he and Gina clung to the idea that Rudy would grow out of it, calm down, settle in.

With the weather warming, they tried leaving him tied to an oak tree in the backyard on a thirty-foot lead. Frustrated at being tied up, Rudy started running in circles around the tree, usually tangling himself until he could hardly move. The family came home to find him bound to the tree, panting and exhausted.

This was dangerous, Sam and Gina both realized; the dog could choke. So after talking to a pet-store proprietor, they reluctantly decided to get Rudy a crate. He almost seemed relieved: this was his own place, the one environment where he couldn't make problems or get into trouble.

Across the street, Diane had incorporated a crate into her puppy's routine from the first because she wanted him to have a safe, secure spot to be alone. Rudy's crate, however, was purchased in desperation. If it made the dog calmer, it also took the family off the hook. It was easy to just leave him there, along with his beloved chewbones, and to shrug off questions of training or bonding. He became what dog walkers called a "crate dog," gotten for unfortunate or impulsive reasons, then confined all day while the family worked or went to school.

Generally, somebody walked Rudy in the morning, or, more likely, just put him out in the backyard. In contrast to Rob's treks with Cherokee in the dark at Mills, these walks were perfunctory. Sam walked the dog to the corner, then back. If Sam was busy, Keith took over and the walk was even shorter. Then Rudy went into the crate and, except for getting sprung briefly by Carmen in the afternoon, stayed there most of the day.

Keith took him for a short walk when he got home around three, if he didn't have soccer practice, a lesson, or plans with friends—and such days were rare. Then it was back in the crate until dinnertime. Afterward, he was allowed to wander around downstairs before bedtime, then crated until the next morning.

The crate did seem to settle him, even if it didn't provide him with stimulation or exercise. In that sense, things got better. Still, the adorable puppy had reached forty pounds. Walks were endurance contests, with Rudy lunging and pulling. He rarely left the house and yard, rarely even went upstairs to the kids' bedrooms. When he did, he plowed into Keith's computer equipment, muddied floors and bedding, annoyed everyone until someone took him downstairs to his crate. Family life flowed around him, vivid and energetic, but he had no connection to any of it. Rudy was attached to no one.

Dogs thrive on attention and reinforcement. Lots of terrific dogs contentedly spend considerable time alone, much of it confined or in crates, but a dog that's often with its owner has a better shot at attachment. It's easier to train, too, since somebody is around to reinforce and correct its behavior. And it probably gets more exercise. Such simple things make dogs happier and easier to live with.

It was poignant to see how it was going with Chaos in his first six months, considering that Rudy was holed up not a hundred yards away.

Like Rudy, Chaos was no accident. A graphic designer who worked at home, Diane took Chaos to nearby Brookdale Park early, before the kids were up. She and her neighbor and friend down the block also took him along on their power walks to Starbucks for coffee a few days a week—their own means of exercise. Chaos was no slouch when it came to energetic walking, but his tongue was nearly dragging by the time this trio got home.

Meanwhile, Diane's trainer came every week for two months. Rain, shine, mud, or snow, Diane and Chaos were out in their front yard every morning and evening for fifteen-minute review sessions.

Diane tried to keep these practices fun, making the sessions short, punctuating their work on "sit" and "lie down" with ball-throwing, treats, and pats. Training wasn't just about the dog's developing good manners; as almost any dog behaviorist will testify, training helps a dog make sense of the human world and function securely and safely within it. A dog made to lie down on command, for example, will almost never confront another dog; nor will other dogs bother it. Training has implications beyond the obvious, and Diane understood this.

For times when Chaos got distracted or rebellious or ignored her commands, she'd learned to give him the silent treatment, turning away or folding her arms. The trainer had explained that dogs love attention, pleasant or not, and that bad behavior could actually be reinforced when people shouted and repeated commands. So when Chaos messed up, Diane looked away and waited thirty seconds, then tried again. When he obliged, he got a biscuit, a hug, or extravagant praise—frequently all three.

There were exceptions. If he headed toward the street or jumped at a stroller, he got a whack on the butt or a reprimand. Either was so unusual that he paid particular attention.

Chaos's crate sat next to the desk in Diane's office. Her work was important to her; she needed to concentrate on it. So Chaos spent several hours dozing there, or chewing on rawhide, and seemed content in her presence. If she had to go out to shop or run errands, he waited in the crate.

"I wanted him to learn to be calm in there," she explained. "That was our deal: I'd give him plenty of attention, exercise, and fun, but he'd be still whenever he was in the crate. If he made noise or whined, I'd ignore him completely. I only responded or spoke to him when he was quiet."

Afternoons, he walked with her or rode in the rear of the minivan while she shopped, ran errands, or picked up the kids. By three, things heated up: there were lessons, games, playdates, dentists' visits. Diane took Chaos along.

Like so many Montclair residents who worked on Wall Street, Phil worked brutal hours and often didn't get home until after dinner. He tried to walk the dog two or three times a week—Diane's idea—so that they would have some kind of relationship. But although Phil and Chaos got on amicably, nobody had any illusions about where the real attachment lay. "She's crazy about that dog," said Phil. "I wouldn't want to mess with that chemistry. I'd get in trouble on both ends."

Sometimes, however, the three of them walked together after dinner, if Phil got home in time. After a few months, Diane had trained Chaos to trot along off-leash, another process that required patience and a firm approach. "I would throw things in front of him, scream 'No street!' even smack the ground with a stick to startle him if he approached the curb." There were more positive ways to accomplish the same thing, but she didn't want to take chances. Chaos picked up on her urgency and stayed reliably on the sidewalk with her and Phil, stopping to sniff trees and shrubs. But if she spotted a child or another dog, or anyone she didn't know, she leashed him. He could look fearsome, with his pointed ears and long legs.

The two of them on their walks made a happy sight, the woman walking briskly, the dog walking by her left knee as if glued there.

"I know I'm lucky because I mostly work at home," Diane acknowledged. "But I don't understand people who won't train their dogs. The dog knows what he's supposed to do and I don't have to scream at him all day. It calms him down to know the rules. I know people are busy, but they'd sure save themselves some time and grief if they did some training. If I weren't home, it might have taken me longer, but I still could have done it, and I would have."

On an early spring afternoon, as Diane walked by, Rudy was barking from the O'Briens' backyard, wagging his tail and straining his tether to get to Chaos. She had a soft spot for a friendly dog, so she went over to toss him a biscuit. She remembered him as a sweet puppy and felt sad that he was so often alone.

Diane and her dog had developed a powerful mutual connection. They loved each other, but as important, they'd found trust, developed communication, and set boundaries. Each knew what the other wanted and didn't, could do and couldn't.

Rudy, for all the O'Briens' good intentions, didn't trust or feel attached to anyone. Perhaps desperate for attention, he overreacted. He leaped up toward Diane as she approached, his big paw dirtying her jacket, the familiar Lab grin on his face. She should have known better: to Chaos, the situation looked nothing but threatening, a dog charging toward him and, more important, toward Diane. Chaos charged and nipped the side of his face. Rudy yelped and jumped back. It was a moment's tension, not a big deal, no real harm done, but it was upsetting.

Diane pulled Chaos away and told him to lie down. He'd never behaved aggressively to another dog, and Rudy seemed such a good-hearted creature. But she understood why Chaos had lunged. Dogs can't always differentiate behavior that's hostile from behavior that's aggressively friendly. She checked to see that Rudy wasn't cut or injured. Chaos, chastened and satisfied that there was no real threat, lay still.

It was an unhappy encounter: Rudy had greeted his neighbors, gotten a biscuit, and been nipped for his troubles. Now, Diane wouldn't put either dog in that situation again, so Rudy had lost potential friends. Again.

As Diane and Chaos moved away, Rudy howled. Perhaps he felt lonely and wanted to repair the social damage. Maybe he wanted to take a walk or get another biscuit. Or maybe he just wanted to run somewhere—anywhere—else.

I'd met plenty of dogs like Rudy in Montclair, lost souls that fell in the gray zone between the abused creatures waiting in the Brooklyn shelter and the well-groomed pets walking through Mills Reservation each morning. They are the casualties of the ways dogs are now acquired and regarded.

The dog-human relationship is complex, resisting absolutes. My own conclusions and perceptions—and much conventional wisdom as well—were continuously being challenged and revised. Dog lovers are always defensively telling themselves and everyone else that they aren't "dog nuts," for instance. But as I spent time with the dogs of Montclair, I noticed the "nuts" often had quite happy dogs and joyous relationships with them, even if baking homemade biscuits seemed excessive. Perhaps the dog nuts should come out of their closets and write their own training manuals.

One of the more surprising studies I read—by Victoria Voith, John Wright, and Peggy Danneman of the Veterinary Hospital of the University of Pennsylvania—challenged the popular wisdom that spoiling and anthropomorphizing dogs necessarily leads to bad behavior.

Owners are frequently advised, these researchers note, that "one should never treat a dog like a person because such dogs will develop serious behavior problems." Letting a dog sleep on the bed or feeding it snacks is verboten, "because such behavior could lead it to misbehave."

Yet this study, published in *Applied Animal Behaviour Science* in 1992, found no evidence to support such fears. "In fact," the authors stress, "dogs taken on trips or [receiving] shared snacks or food from the table were significantly *less* likely to engage in behavior problems."

This was surprising at first. Perhaps the researchers were really saying that people whose dogs are deeply attached to them—who take their dogs along and share food—are likely to have dogs that are calmer and more responsive.

Diane hadn't thought much about it, but when I asked, she conceded that her own childhood had been dreary. Her parents were unhappily preoccupied with economic survival, and there was little warmth or fun in the house. Her father wasn't around much; her mother was critical and demanding.

"You never felt you worked hard enough for her. Never did well enough in school. Never looked quite right. Until I was an adult, I believed she hated me. Now I realize she loves me quite a bit, but she felt overwhelmed and she worried that I wouldn't be tough enough for the world. And, let's face it, she had no idea how to be a parent. She certainly hid her love for us."

Chaos demonstrated his love constantly. Every time Diane spoke to him, his tail wagged. He showed all the behaviors of an attached dog: he looked her in the eye, he responded when she said his name, and he was faithfully, if not instantly, obedient. He strolled beside her, sat when told, came when called. He had his imperfections—she'd learned not to leave the kitchen while a roast or a chicken was cooling on a countertop—but that was the way she wanted it. "To make him snap to instantly, I'd have to do things I don't really want to," she felt. "He does what I need him to do."

Perhaps because she'd grown up with too much discipline and too little love, she'd found a better balance with her dog—gentle, even-handed discipline and instruction, along with the kind of affection and approval she herself craved. Chaos had benefited. So had she. In ways she found she couldn't quite articulate, this relationship had proven surprisingly healthy for her, she said.

Rudy, meanwhile, was another story. Montclair was a community that raised its children with a vengeance. Middle-class kids there got all the things children were supposed to get—good schools, music lessons and sports, rides all over town to play with their friends, refrigerators obscured behind sheaves of their artwork and marathon schedules. For many parents, dogs were a part of that package, included in the snapshot in their heads as they left Brooklyn or the Upper West Side for the suburbs.

Rudy wasn't acquired to provide love or emotional support, to do the new work of dogs. He was purchased much like an iMac or a skateboard, something special for a kid at Christmas, a loving, loyal creature to accompany a boy through childhood, whether the boy needed companionship or not.

It's also possible that a little more advance work might have resulted in a happier experience. Breeds vary dramatically. Although they're beautiful and even-tempered, the big, powerful hunting and working dogs need the most exercise and work.

Smaller breeds—Maltese, bichon frise, Wheaton, and West Highland terriers—are smart, affectionate, highly trainable dogs who need comparatively little exercise. They're much more suitable for busy urban or suburban families. But in Montclair, they are far outnumbered—three to one, according to town records—by the bigger, more energetic working and hunting breeds.

Sam said he decided on a Lab because he kept seeing them on television and in magazine ads and was struck by how beautiful they were.

Accompanying a dog walker on her rounds through Montclair, something I'd done on and off for several months, I found versions of Rudy all over town: big, strong working dogs with no work to do. Loving creatures eager to attach to humans, they found nobody—literally—at home. The dog walker struggled to control them on their outings; they strained, frantic and hyper, as if they knew they'd better make the most of the little outdoors time they had.

As Chaos demonstrated, working dogs didn't necessarily need to herd sheep or retrieve game. They could be quite content doing things that approximate work—chasing balls or Frisbees, sniffing their way through parks or down streets, hanging around with people who love them. Without that, they were frequently in trouble.

Day by day, Rudy lolled in his crate or circled his tree; he seemed more distant every time I saw him. At some point, say people who know dogs well, he would give up. It seemed at times that the soulfulness had already vanished from his dark eyes.

CHAPTER 9

AIN'T SHE A DOLL?

Most afternoons, Tom Fogarty and Penny could be found standing by the athletic-field fence, across from his neatly tended house with the American flag and the potted plants, watching the high school teams practice. Tom was outside almost every day between three and six. No matter the weather, he wore a cap, sport shirt, and gray trousers, and he moved slowly and painfully, his back stooped, his knees slightly bent, Penny's leash in one hand and a cane in the other.

His wife of fifty-two years was gone now; she died of cancer some years ago. "My kids is all gone, too," Tom added, whistling through the wide gap between his upper front teeth. He had three children, but "they moved away from here, and I don't get to see 'em that much."

Tom was vague about his age but conceded with a grin that he was fast moving toward eighty. He still worked, though, driving a few miles in his beat-up old Buick to a service station where he pumped gas a few hours four mornings a week.

It was hard to actually have a conversation with Tom. He constantly peered to the left and right, and if he saw someone approaching, he retreated across the street, pulling a shorthaired, pointy-headed dog who never stopped wagging her tail and rarely stopped barking.

Penny, at first glance, looked almost as old as Tom. Short and squat, she had some dental problems and bare patches on her back and legs. She'd been covered in mange when his daughter dropped her off three years ago. Betsy was moving to Seattle, Tom said, and she couldn't bear the thought of leaving him all by himself. So she paid a visit to PAWS, the local animal shelter, where she adopted the dog, then surprised her father by bringing her to his front door. Tom recalls warmly that Penny tried to chew his leg off at their first encounter, "but her teeth aren't so good." It was, he said, love at first sight.

Penny had been left tied to the door of the local animal shelter in the middle of the night. PAWS told me they kept Penny for eighteen months, and that except for a retired schoolteacher who brought her back after one day because she wouldn't stop barking, no one had shown any interest in adopting her.

"I never had a dog. My wife liked cats. But before my daughter moved away, she came over one day and just dropped her off with a bowl and a leash. She said, 'Dad, I just can't stand you being alone.'" Of course, added Tom, Penny had been alone, too.

"I don't know why," he said, "but we just got along right off. Like we'd been together for years."

Penny scratched at her neck, and barked furiously, spittle flying from her nearly toothless mouth.

"Ain't she a doll?" Tom beamed.

Penny wasn't one of those dogs in TV commercials. She didn't have doe eyes. She wasn't cute. She performed no tricks, obeyed no commands, showed no affection toward or interest in anyone but Tom. And, like him, she walked slowly and unsteadily.

Unlike Tom, Penny was loud. She yapped at every car and person that approached. She disliked other dogs, jumping and snapping at them when she could get close enough. In fact, the reason Tom hobbled off when he saw someone coming, he explained, was because he feared people would call the police if she made too much noise, and the cops would take Penny away. Besides, his landlord didn't know that Tom had a dog.

He lived well outside the various subcultures that made up the dog-owning and -loving world in Montclair. He lived on the ground floor of an asbestos-shingled duplex in a working-class pocket near the municipal garage. One day soon, I was sure, his landlord would cash in and sell the duplex to one of the newcomers with money. It had happened all over town. There weren't many people left in Montclair who pumped gas for a living.

Tom didn't know about obedience classes, or positive reinforcement. He didn't go to pet stores for rawhide chews or fleecy beds. He didn't own a ball or a Frisbee for Penny to chase, and her demeanor indicated that the very suggestion would tick her off.

But it was hard to imagine an animal who illustrated as well as Penny what dogs and people can mean to one another at certain points in their lives, and just how varied the new work of dogs is. In another place or time, Tom would have been living with relatives, or surrounded by neighbors who'd known him for years and looked out for him. Now, his family scattered and his town changing around him, there was just Penny.

Their world was bounded by his patio, a small front lawn, and the stretch of chain-link fence along the football field where he tied Penny while he watched the high school teams practice, season after season, and she barked at the players, the coaches, the whistles, the other people standing by the fence to watch. She also barked at passing trucks and cyclists, and various unseen sounds and smells.

Their routine began there each morning, as Tom walked Penny along the fence. They never ventured more than a house or two beyond Tom's. He was afraid to take her to the park down the street, where she might run away or fight with other dogs, or maybe bark too loudly and scare kids. It wasn't clear she could even make it that far.

Then breakfast. Tom had cereal and toast and gave his aging cat half a can of tuna. Penny got the other half, growling at me between mouthfuls.

"Shhhhh, now," Tom murmured over and over. "Sssssh, now. Aw, c'mon, Penny, be nice."

He was constantly apologizing for her, exhorting her to calm down, to be polite and friendly. At each plea, she looked lovingly at Tom, wagged her tail, and barked on.

"She's all I have now," he told me. "Everyone else is gone.

"She can be a doll, especially to some of the women neighbors," Tom assured me. "She'll wag her tail and lick them. But she doesn't like men much, or other dogs." Actually, he admitted, she wasn't even all that crazy about most women, except for his next-door neighbor, who brought dinner leftovers outside and left them in a bowl beside their common driveway.

Penny had never bitten a person, or even another dog, but Tom's dread of that was palpable. He couldn't be dissuaded from the notion that any day, somebody would come by and take Penny ("Penny . . . because she's copper-colored") back to the shelter.

After breakfast, Tom headed to work at the gas station. Often Penny came along to sit in his Buick and bark at the customers. Otherwise, she stayed behind in his musty living room—hung with pictures of his late wife, his kids, and of Tom with some army buddies—and stared out the window. A passerby could always tell if Penny was at home, because of the din from within.

Who were the soldiers? Tom just waved his hand.

"They're all gone." He didn't want to dredge it up.

Tom's house was a bit of a period piece, with its fifties linoleum floors, wood paneling, and fading sofas and chairs. One of the chairs was Penny's, although she was technically forbidden to jump up on the furniture. "I keep telling her to get off of it." He shrugged. "But she don't listen to me. You can see that." You could. But she didn't take her eyes from him, either.

When Tom came home from work, he tidied up, took out the garbage, walked Penny along the fence, then took up position on his front stoop, Penny's clothesline leash tied to his chair. "I don't take no chances with her, 'cause she'll misbehave as quick as anything. . . ."

After several hours of watching and barking at passersby and traffic, waving to neighbors, shushing the dog, cajoling, scolding, and more barking—"C'mon, now, Penny, can't you be quiet and nice?"—the two went inside for dinner, often chicken or hamburger, sometimes a sandwich or a frozen dinner Tom heated up.

Penny got half of everything, including salad and

dessert, and Tom was meticulous about the fifty-fifty split. He put her bowl on the kitchen table and divided everything with an old porcelain-handled knife. Then he put her bowl on the floor next to him, and turned on the TV in the next room so he could hear the news.

Penny scarfed down her food greedily, growling and snapping between mouthfuls, spewing food all over the floor, while Tom ate slowly, deliberately, chatting with her. "Atta girl, eat up. You like that?" And to me, "Ain't she a doll?"

He took Penny for her last walk of the day, across the street to the fence, before the two settled in for an evening of TV. "My eyes aren't so good, so I can't see everything clear but I can listen, because my hearing is real good."

Penny left her chair to jump up on the sofa and curl next to Tom. Like him, she was getting tired.

Where did she sleep?

"Well, she's not allowed on the bed," Tom said quickly. "But sometimes, she just does get up there—though, like me, she's not all that spry." It was true. Sometimes Penny looked up at a bed or sofa, but seemed to conclude it was too much trouble.

It took me a few visits to see the kind of work Penny was doing, and how seriously she took her responsibilities—keeping Tom company, keeping him safe.

One quiet evening when Penny had eased her vigilance and gone to sleep on the patio, Tom hinted that he wasn't "all that healthy," that he tired easily at his gas-station job. He might be ill, he suggested, might need some form of medical treatment. He didn't volunteer any specifics. But he worried about what would happen to Penny if anything happened to him. He wondered if I might like to take her in; he nodded when, reasonably enough, I pointed out that she wouldn't get along with my border collies. I doubted he really wanted to think about life without her, anyway. "I didn't want her at first," he told me (again), almost in wonder at such an idea. "Didn't ever have a dog. But now . . . well, I don't know what I would do without her. She's everything, just everything, to me."

They sat a while, her head inches from Tom's feet; the fireflies blinking around them, the traffic sounds from the street more occasional. Penny dreamed, growling. Tom, grateful for the chance to love her as much as he did, watched her fondly.

"My daughter says I'll probably have to go into a nursing home or one of those facilities," he offered, reaching down to pat the dog. "I can't go, not while Penny's alive." And then a mischievous smile. "And I don't need to go at all. We're all right here."

Penny woke up, saw me as if for the first time, and barked furiously. "Oh, hush," Tom

221

cajoled. Exhausted, she quieted down, keeled over, and was soon asleep again, snoring loudly. Tom stroked her head and she growled gently in her sleep.

CHAPTER 10

TRIXIE'S TIME

Angela Giamatti celebrated her seventy-eighth birthday as she had celebrated the last ten since her best friend, Grace, died: alone in her apartment on Walnut Street with her miniature poodle, Trixie, who'd turned seventeen a few days earlier. But her girls checked in.

The older daughter, Maria, called a little before noon from Tucson, where she lived with her husband and two children, to wish her mother a happy birthday and see how she was doing. Maria always wanted to come out and help her celebrate; but she always said no.

Tina, the younger one, usually called at night. She worked for Microsoft in Seattle. "They plan it," Mrs. Giamatti explained. "One calls me in the morning, and one at night, so I won't be lonely. They think I haven't noticed."

Judging from the photos on the polished mahogany table in the living room, Mrs. Giamatti and Trixie had both been lookers years ago. Mrs. Giamatti once was a wire-thin brunette with a spirited twinkle in her eye. Trixie was an elegant white furball with much the same Jersey Girl élan—big hair enhanced by a blue ribbon perched over one ear.

Time, however, had worn both of them down. Mrs. Giamatti had been through two hip replacements and took a pile of pills for arthritis, mild diabetes, and high blood pressure. She looked frail, a little hunched. Still, she took meticulous care of herself. Her hair was frosted to a bluish-white sheen, and she wore an aqua pantsuit and a small gold crucifix.

Trixie had been struggling with kidney disease for several years and had recently been diagnosed with stomach cancer. She was wan and thin, her coat mottled and yellowed, her eyes rheumy, her teeth stained. Mostly, she lay curled on a round dog bed in the living room, next to Mrs. Giamatti's favorite green easy chair.

"We've always been easy together. She's never been any trouble," Mrs. Giamatti said ruefully. "Now we both spend half of our lives at doctors' offices."

Getting Trixie to the vet was no simple matter for a near-octogenerian with bad hips. Mrs. Giamatti had to get the cardboard carrier out of the hall closet (crates were too heavy and, anyway, Trixie hated them), call the cab company, and pay the driver extra to carry Trixie down into the taxi and then into the vet's office. And when it was time to come home, the whole process had to be repeated in reverse. A neighbor had recommended a vet who visited the elderly with a mobile van, but that proved too expensive. Besides, Trixie had been going to Dr. Brenda King forever.

Still, it was hard. Even in her feeble state, Trixie wasn't crazy about being confined in a cardboard box, nor did she like being toted around by strangers. Until a few years ago "she might have put a small hole or two" in anybody who tried to carry her out, said Mrs. Giamatti. But that was a younger, more vigorous Trixie; she'd since grown too weak to make any trouble.

In fact, it had been two days since Trixie had eaten anything, and she was hardly moving, unwilling even to take a short stroll. This was a change, one that Dr. King had talked to her about.

So Mrs. Giamatti made an appointment for Trixie the next morning at eight. She said she expected to come home from the vet's alone.

It was, it seemed, Trixie's time.

Until a year or so ago, while Trixie could still hop up onto the broad window ledge, the two of them liked to gaze out at the traffic, the neighbors walking their own dogs, the comings and goings at the township's municipal building down the street.

The five-story brick apartment building was handy to downtown shopping and a supermarket, and two tiny parks nearby were perfect for a small poodle to sniff around in and take care of her business. Although the building seemed ripe for a rehab aimed at attracting the town's burgeoning population of hip singles, it was for now what sociologists call a NORC—a naturally occurring retirement community, too musty for young professionals, too small for middle-class families, but a natural for the elderly who didn't want to leave town and weren't yet ready for assisted living.

Mrs. Giamatti lived mostly in two rooms—the spacious living room and her bedroom—but the apartment had three more: a fifties-style kitchen, a second bedroom for the kids when they visited, and a dining room she never used but had decorated with pictures of her family.

None of them knew of the impending vet visit. Mrs. Giamatti hadn't told Maria that Trixie was getting sicker, and was likely to be put down soon. That could wait. She knew how Maria would grieve. She also felt it was "very personal," something between her and the dog.

"Maria loved this dog so much," Mrs. Giamatti remembered. "When she had troubles with her husband, she came home and spent a week just holding Trixie in her lap." That the marital problems were happily resolved had always seemed to them to have something to do with the presence of the little dog.

Besides, Maria would worry even more about her mother being alone. Guilty about living so far away, she was comforted by the fact that the vigilant Trixie was still around when everyone else was gone. Mrs. Giamatti did nothing to encourage her daughter's feelings of guilt; she thought it was a sad world where children lived so far from their parents, but she also understood it was the nature of the world now. There was nothing to do about it.

Still, Trixie's passing would have implications, Mrs. Giamatti herself understood. Her last significant reason for staying in the apartment alone was probably about to evaporate.

"In a way, I'm ready," she sighed. "In another, I'm not." She wanted to think it all through before it became a topic of familial conversation. Trixie had been a bulwark against that.

When I first came in, Trixie got up, circled me briefly, yipped once, then went back to a fitful, uneasy sleep. Mrs. Giamatti smiled at this sign of the formerly feisty old Trix.

It was a funny thing about small dogs: they often seemed fearless, as if they had no idea how small they really were. Like Trixie, they could project an air of authority, as if they were in charge. As a result, people and other dogs often assumed that they *were* in charge. It's common to see a pug or bichon frise push a rottweiler or a German shepherd around. Even in her weakened state, Trixie could summon this royal imperiousness, woofing contemptuously at noises in the hallway, or at a passing siren.

Until recently, Trixie spent most of her days in Mrs. Giamatti's lap, supervising the world. These days, Mrs. Giamatti hired a teenager from her church to take Trixie out some mornings and evenings, especially in rain or snow, since walking had become painful for both of them. But on warm or sunny days, if she were feeling well and her hip didn't hurt too badly, she and Trixie made their way laboriously out of the apartment, into the elevator, down to the street, and toward the small park where the two of them could sit on a bench, take the air, and maybe chat with some of Mrs. Giamatti's friends. Only two or three remained in the neighborhood.

"The others, they're all gone or in nursing homes," she said softly, shaking her head. "Just a few of us left, and we don't go out that much." None of them were big "phone yakkers," so life could get lonely. Trixie made a difference.

Angela Giamatti came from a culture that didn't talk much about feelings—for dogs or for people—although women could always be expected to coo about their children. At the mention of her daughters or grandchildren, Mrs. Giamatti grew animated, pointed out photographs, almost glowed.

"When you get to my point in life, what really matters?" she asked, sipping a cup of tea, which she took straight, no milk or sugar. "You're always too hot, too cold, too tired, and something hurts, and you have a lot of time to look back. You know you have a lot of time in the past and not much time at all in the future. God willing, it will not be hard when I go.

"But what do you look back on? Family. I look back on family. Trixie is part of that family that used to live here, and she's all I have left now. I love my children very much, but they have their own lives—and they *should* have their own lives. Trixie is still here, bless her."

Even now she didn't like to complain. Everybody had problems, many worse than hers, and problems were part of life. She had been blessed, and was grateful for what she had.

She was born in Newark, as was her husband, Vincent, who'd put in thirty-five years in the Montclair Department of Public Works. She believed she ought to be at home until her two daughters graduated from high school; after that, she took a secretarial job in the Montclair Public Schools. They had moved into this apartment—with Trixie, whom Vincent also adored—after they both retired. (He died of kidney disease not long afterward.)

Deeply religious, she had made it to church every Sunday until her hip surgeries. Now she went to mass perhaps once a month. "But you can pray at home," she said, and there was a portrait of Jesus hanging in the living room. Father Joseph came to see her now and then, a much-appreciated kindness.

She missed her daughters terribly, but would never tell them so, because they already felt bad enough about having moved away. "No mother could ask for more," she announced. "Good husbands who have good jobs, wonderful children, thank God. Beautiful homes. All my prayers have been answered, only I wish Vincent could have been here to see the grandchildren grow up."

There were four of them, and it wasn't possible to count the numbers of photos of them, from birth through young adulthood, on every tabletop and wall in the apartment—babies at the beach, kids at birthday parties, teenagers at Disney World. If Maria and Tina couldn't be with their mother often, they could at least make sure that Mrs. Giamatti missed nothing of importance in their lives.

She had maintained a disciplined routine even after she stopped working, even after Vincent's death, and Trixie had always been an integral part of it. There were her three walks a day with Trixie, volunteer work at the church, lunch with friends. She made the occasional excursion (before the hip troubles) to Atlantic City to blow five dollars in quarters at the slots, and two or three trips a year (boarding Trixie with Dr. King) to see her daughters and their families, hosting them in return every year around the holidays. It had in some ways been a pleasant, peaceful time.

Trixie was always there, in many of the pictures, for many of the moments. Trixie had marked with her some of her most important milestones.

She remembered the dog waiting at home for

her after Vincent died at Mountainside Hospital; she remembered Trixie comforting her after Maria moved west, then Tina. She remembered how patient Trixie was when she started walking again after hip surgery, and she remembered the walk they took together after her best friend, Grace, died of ovarian cancer.

The poodle had become deeply important, yet Mrs. Giamatti came from a different generation and had a particular sensibility that didn't anthropomorphize pets. She never spoke about Trixie the same way she talked about her children or grandchildren. She rarely assumed that she knew what the poodle was thinking, or that it might be thinking at all, nor did she talk to her, at least out loud, about her problems.

This reluctance to see the dog as human didn't mean she wasn't utterly devoted to her, didn't dread losing her, didn't spoil her rotten. Trixie ate two meals a day, a small can of dog food each morning and a wide variety of home-cooked Italian dishes at night; her favorite was spaghetti vongole. But otherwise, the distinction between Trixie as companion animal and Trixie as something more seemed clear.

By now, I'd seen that people loved dogs for all sorts of reasons—Rob cherished his silent companion Cherokee as did Sandra the little dachshund who gave her the chance to feel like a mother. For Mrs. Giamatti, the importance of a dog wasn't the surrogate work it did but the

231

passages of life it had come to represent. Trixie was a link; when Mrs. Giamatti saw her, she saw not only a beloved pet but a husband, visiting children, a life. There was that blank canvas again.

In Albert and Bulcroft's 1988 study "Pets, Families, and the Life Course," the researchers found that pet ownership is comparatively low among widowed people for a number of reasons: physical frailty, expense, housing restrictions, and a desire for autonomy. Many older people in Montclair also told me they didn't want to get a dog that would almost surely outlive them.

But for those widowed or single people who own one, a pet can be an important source of affection and companionship. "As givers and receivers of affection," note Albert and Bulcroft, "pets can contribute to the morale maintenance of people who live alone or with few significant others to play such roles." And, compared to other animals, the researchers found, dogs are the most adept at playing affectionate and emotionally supportive roles.

Angela Giamatti smiled when I read this to her, and shook her head. She had no idea what "morale maintenance" meant, and it wasn't an idea she wanted to explore much. "Trixie keeps me company, and keeps me busy," she said.

Since Vincent died, it's been me and Trixie, and we've done okay. She's good company, she's a good girl. Hey, Trixie?" At this, Trixie climbed laboriously out of her bed, walked over to sit between Mrs. Giamatti's legs, and wagged her tail. Then she went back and lay down again. She looked miserable.

If not for Trixie, Mrs. Giamatti would probably have heeded her daughters' pleadings and moved into a Catholic assisted-living home in Union County a year or two ago, after her health problems intensified.

She knew Maria and Tina were uneasy with her being alone; she wasn't crazy about it herself. Every day, it seemed, the little things got harder. She was clearheaded about the idea that she couldn't live independently for much longer, let alone take care of an aging dog. But she didn't want to leave Montclair, wouldn't consider any facility that meant giving Trixie away, and she wouldn't put Trixie down before her time.

More than one Montclair vet had lamented to me about the suffering and enormous cost of dogs that people refused to euthanize, but Mrs. Giamatti was a realist. She didn't want the dog to suffer, and if Trixie couldn't eat pasta or walk . . . well, Dr. King had told her that was when it would be time. "Sometimes it takes more love *not* to force them to live," she said, quoting the vet. She thought that was right.

But it wasn't clear if she grasped how difficult the next few weeks and months might be. Bereavement reactions following the death of a close friend or relative have been well documented, as Kenneth

Keddie noted in the *British Journal of Psychiatry* in 1977, while the connection between domestic animals, loss, and mental health has been largely ignored by psychiatry.

Keddie found that the loss of a dog or cat sometimes hit people as hard as the loss of a limb or a home, resulting in acute depression, agitation, and other types of "psychiatric penalty."

The next morning, a spring Thursday that promised to be bright and breezy, Mrs. Giamatti got up early, dressed, bent her head in prayer beneath the portrait of Jesus, put on a pot of coffee, and took Trixie out for a short walk.

It was difficult for her to bend over and put a leash on the dog, who came quietly to her side when she called but remained distracted, listless, without appetite.

The two slowly made their way down the hallway, into the elevator, down to the ground floor, out the lobby, and onto the landscaped triangle in front of the entranceway.

Trixie stopped and lay down. "Come on, girl, let's go. We have to try." A few times lately, when the weather was stormy or either she or Trixie felt particularly bad, Mrs. Giamatti had put newspapers down in the kitchen for Trixie. She thought it must be embarrassing for the dog and felt bad for her. This time, Trixie piddled against a shrub, and they went back upstairs.

At seven-thirty, a brown-and-white taxi, an

enormous old Chevy that looked as if it had a million miles on it, pulled up to the building. The cab company added five dollars to the fare on account of the dog. The driver hopped out, came upstairs, helped Mrs. Giamatti get the dog into the cardboard carrier, and brought it downstairs with no protest from Trixie. Getting into the cab wasn't easy for Mrs. Giamatti, either, who took it one step at a time, leaning heavily against the car door and the driver.

She'd put on her church clothes, a dark-brown dress and jacket, and, even though they hurt her feet, her brown pumps; she carried a shopping bag.

When the cab reached Dr. King's office a few minutes later—I followed in my car—Mrs. Giamatti waited until the driver came around to help her out. A vet's assistant came out to carry Trixie, in her box, straight into the vet's office while Mrs. Giamatti came deliberately up the steps. She and the dog exchanged anxious glances as the assistant took her into an examining room. Mrs. Giamatti was ushered right inside.

Dr. King was already examining the nearly limp poodle, looking at her eyes, checking her heartbeat, taking her temperature. She closed the door behind Mrs. Giamatti to speak with her alone.

When the door opened, ten minutes later, Mrs. Giamatti had opened her shopping bag. She'd brought along a photo of her late husband, her two daughters, and four grandchildren. She'd also brought a picture—the only one she had—of the whole family with Trixie, taken on the last visit when they were all together.

She was holding on to her composure. "I've been to a lot of funerals," she said. "I'm not going to lose it here." Not in public. Not in a vet's office.

"Dr. King says it's time," she said. King, a no-nonsense, respected local vet, nodded soberly. The dog was going into kidney failure, she said, and the cancer would soon kill her anyway. King believed that dog owners who loved their dogs knew when to put them down, and when they decided to proceed, she tried to treat them and the occasion with dignity, saying little and moving quickly.

Mrs. Giamatti placed her framed pictures along the edge of the examining table, "so Trixie can see the people who loved her."

The dog was barely conscious, but she crawled next to the old woman, nuzzled her hand, and closed her eyes. Dr. King asked Mrs. Giamatti if she wanted a few minutes alone with the dog. She said no, just felt for her crucifix, put it to her lips, and then put her hand on the dog's head as Dr. King administered the anesthesia, and then, a few minutes later, the powerful second injection that would quickly stop the dog's heart.

It was over in seconds, it seemed. Trixie never moved, or even opened her eyes, and when Dr. King checked for a heartbeat with a stethoscope, she shook her head. It was done.

She said she was sorry, patted Mrs. Giamatti's arm, and left the room. Mrs. Giamatti faltered a bit; her eyes teared. She had asked for the dog to be cremated, with the ashes to be returned to her, though she wasn't precisely sure what she would do with them. When she got home, she would call Maria and Tina, and give them the news. Or maybe she'd wait a day. She was very tired, she said.

Mrs. Giamatti collected the pictures, put them back into her shopping bag, then turned to the lifeless Trixie on the examining table. "Goodbye, girl," she said, then turned around and walked away. She had forgotten all about paying for the procedure, but Dr. King whispered hurriedly to her assistant not to worry about it.

I took Mrs. Giamatti to Our Lady of the Cross—she didn't utter a word during the drive—and waited outside while she visited briefly with Father Joseph, who walked her back out the front entrance and said he would come by the next day. He said he was sorry.

She told me she'd lit a candle for Trixie and said a prayer for her loyal, loving soul. "And one for myself," she added, quietly. She thought she would see Trixie again, and Father Joseph had agreed.

Back on Walnut Street, Mrs. Giamatti struggled to get out of the car. Then, carrying her bag of pictures, she walked slowly, on my arm, into her lobby. She nodded to a neighbor, pushed the elevator button, walked stiffly down her hallway, and unlocked the door to her apartment. She hesitated for perhaps four or five seconds before turning the key and opening the door.

After hanging up her jacket she went into the kitchen to heat some water for tea. When it was ready she sat down in her green stuffed chair. She looked steady and composed, but utterly spent. And she looked around, then down at the dog bed on the floor.

People sometimes suffer enormous grief and pain when they lose their dogs, and it can be difficult for more than the obvious reasons. They feel embarrassed to mourn animals too deeply or too openly, so they often keep their emotions to themselves. Mrs. Giamatti seemed to be one of those.

People who have lost dogs often tell of expecting to see them in familiar settings weeks or even months later; Mrs. Giamatti would be startled for some time to look down and not see Trixie lying beside her.

She was going to leave the poodle's bed next to her chair for a while before getting rid of it, she said. Later on, she would clear out Trixie's food, leashes, and toys. She would call her daughters with the news and brace herself for whatever came next.

EPILOGUE

DOGVILLE, REVISITED

Last september I brought my two border collies, Homer and Devon, to a sheepherding demonstration at a Scottish and Irish Festival, held at a recreational preserve in eastern Pennsylvania. For my friend Carolyn Wilki, who was my dog trainer and herding instructor, as well as the herder for the fair, these demo days were gruelingly long. They began around dawn at her Raspberry Ridge Sheep Farm, when she took her flock out to graze. Then she hustled to round up dogs, wrestle half a dozen recalcitrant sheep into her pickup, and load the fenceposts necessary to set up a small pen at the fair.

By the time she pulled out of her driveway, her truck resembled something out of Rube Goldberg, fenceposts lashed to the cap, sheep tucked inside around bales of hay, tanks of water and crates of dogs all connected by bungee cords.

Payment for this trek came to peanuts—maybe several hundred dollars for two dawn-to-dusk days, one of them hot, the other rainy—but Carolyn accepted almost every invitation she got,

239

demonstrating sheepherding up and down the East Coast. She believed she was helping the public to appreciate this ancient skill, and showing them dogs at their best.

It seemed a noble effort, so now and then, the dogs and I went along to help out. Using an amplifier and a mike that sometimes functioned, I narrated the "action," as Carolyn—wearing a clan badge, a sash, kilt, and tam-o'-shanter, and calling herself Carolyn MacWilki for the occasion—put her dogs and sheep through their paces. Then my dogs got to show off a little, too.

These fairs, usually patched-together, nonprofit affairs, were wildly popular, especially among parents of small kids desperate for something wholesome to do on weekends. The fairs seemed to keep notions of ethnicity and cultural variety alive; in a homogenizing world, they were a way of reminding people where they came from.

I'd come to expect certain staples of the Irish and Scottish fairs: blue-collar sightseers, bagpipers and hurlers, folk bands and flutists, a few raggedy craft booths selling leprechaun pottery and carved walking sticks, and tents serving meat pies and fish and chips while somewhere discreetly in the background other vendors did a brisk business in hot dogs and pizza.

But the sheepherding was always a featured event. Border collies were specially bred more than a century ago in Ireland and Scotland to corral, collect, and move sheep from barns to windswept pastures and moors, and back again. Now, on farms or in small parks or school playing fields, they re-created that work. At least five hundred people showed up for our three herding demonstrations that Saturday, rushing to stake out the best vantage points, setting up lawn chairs, pulling out cameras and video recorders, telling their kids and friends how they'd seen herding on the Discovery Channel and wouldn't it be fun to watch in real life?

Each demonstration lasted about half an hour. Carolyn, who practically glowed with delight at demonstrating this ancient art, released her sheep, sent a dog to drive them several hundred yards up a grassy hill, then sent another on a wide sweep—an "outrun"—to fetch the sheep and bring them back to the pen.

Her chief herding dog, Dave, himself a Scotsman, was generally, and deservedly, the star, driving the sheep as Carolyn gave voice and whistle commands and I explained to the audience what was going on.

Though a simple exercise by herding standards, something about the dog tearing up the hill to control the sheep touched the spectators. They murmured excitedly at the way Carolyn could make dogs she could barely see turn left or right, circle around, or drop down onto the grass as if they were remote-controlled. Her dogs were focused and lightning-quick; the sheep baahed atmospherically and grabbed as much grass as they could.

"Lord," breathed one of the women in the morning audience. "And here I've been trying for nine years to get Girlie to just sit down."

At activities like weaving and hurling, the crowd drifted away once the demo ended. But after the sheepherding, spectators descended upon Carolyn almost as a single unit. They told her how much they admired the dogs, how they'd love to work with such animals. Some had seen border collies and other herding breeds work before, in Europe or on western ranches. They'd never forget it, they'd said. Amazing. They seemed to find Carolyn's dogs, and even mine, exotic creatures. They sounded wistful about them.

Given the range of entertainment most American families had at their disposal, watching these odd, hyper little dogs race after sheep didn't seem all that gripping. But maybe that was the point. Maybe the people were touched by seeing something they'd missed—a time when people and dogs were essential to one another in practical, as well as emotional, ways.

Herding intrigued them, I thought, because, as one woman said, "It sort of reminds me why there are dogs, where they came from, how long they've been helping us out."

For whatever reason, as the sheep rushed up and down the hill, pausing whenever they could to nibble grass, as Carolyn blew her whistle and shouted "Come by" and "Away to me" and "That'll do!" and as the dogs moved the flock along, the crowd oohed and aaaaahed as if watching a space launch.

My dogs enjoyed a bit of reflected glory. Almost everyone reached down to touch them or called to them. Homer was affable but indifferent; he lived for sheep. He'd spend the entire day by their pen, never taking his eyes off them, waiting for his turn to herd. Devon, high-strung, hung by my side, as usual.

By the third and final demo, we were all dragging a bit, even the dogs. The early fall sun was still strong and the air sultry; there was no shade. Homer was sitting by the fence, waiting to go on.

A small squadron of bagpipers—their music announced that the herding event was about to begin—were moving past an enormous man in a kilt who was tossing what looked like a telephone pole over his shoulder. (Later I found out it *was* a telephone pole.)

As I readied my balky microphone, a small yellow van pulled up the service driveway, wound slowly through the crowd, and parked just behind my truck. Two middle-aged women in jeans and sneakers hopped out and opened the side doors.

A small group of kids from a residence for disabled children climbed or were helped out. A few were seriously physically handicapped; others were severely retarded; three were in wheelchairs. The crowd made way.

One of the children being wheeled toward us—I soon learned that his name was Joey and that he was twelve—spotted Devon and began to shout. His words weren't clear. "Dog! Dog!" is what I thought he was saying, and he seemed not frightened but excited. His round face was framed by blond hair, and he was wearing a weathered brown baseball cap, dark blue sneakers, jeans, and a Mickey Mouse T-shirt. He was clutching a frayed stuffed animal and he was making a lot of noise.

Though the teacher pushing his chair tried to quiet him, he kept calling to the dog. With Devon still yards away, by my side, Joey began to get frustrated, pounding the arms of the chair and kicking out with his feet.

I quickly stepped in front of Devon. Border collies can get aroused by sudden, herky-jerky motions. Owners of the breed share stories of their odd, sometimes unfriendly natures, of unhappy encounters with toddlers, cyclists, skateboarders, and cars, all of which can trigger the herding instinct and sometimes a frightening response. The very things the crowd most loved to see at demonstrations—herding dogs giving chase after noisy things moving away from them—can also be dangerous.

Besides, Devon had a complicated history; he was excitable and unpredictable. Although he had never been aggressive, when I first took him in he would shy away from kids, jumping when one or two grabbed at him or took him by surprise. Carolyn and I had spent two years working to desensitize him to noises and sudden movements, to calm him down. We had largely succeeded, yet I had no idea how he might react to the highly animated Joey.

But Devon walked straight over to the boy, hesitated for just a moment, then put his head in Joey's lap. Then he crawled *into* Joey's lap.

As if a switch had been turned off, Joey calmed almost instantly, as Devon sat completely still. The teacher, looking delighted, whispered into Joey's ear and, guiding his hand, showed him how to stroke the dog's back. Two people in the crowd pointed their video cameras at the dog and the boy, as if they were part of the demonstration. I moved closer, not sure what to do.

Devon began to slurp at Joey's face. The boy laughed and shrieked with pleasure. I gestured to Carolyn to take a look at what was going on; she grinned.

But Joey grabbed Devon tighter, squeezing him and saying, "Mii-ne. Mii-ne." Devon stiffened. I spoke to him in a soothing voice, moving toward him, but deliberately. If the teacher intervened, or if I rushed up, things could get worse. Joey could get too rough; Devon might grow alarmed.

I told Joey the dog's name and he began chanting "Dev-on," "Dev-on"—only he pronounced it "De-*thon*," emphasizing the second syllable, almost shouting. He was still clutching Devon as if he were a teddy bear, something few dogs like, particularly from an excited stranger. But after his initial surprise, Devon appeared at ease. It was not what I would have expected.

As I reached the scene, Charlene introduced herself as Joey's teacher; she was beaming. "Joey hasn't talked much these last few months. It's been a tough time for him; he's relatively new with us. He loves your dog. Is it okay?"

It looked okay, for the moment.

Devon was still, his tail swishing contentedly. Something unusual was happening, I slowly realized. This was a different kind of work for my working dog.

I couldn't quite explain it. Maybe Joey had spilled food on his shirt. Perhaps Devon was responding to his focused attention and affection. Perhaps he sensed a need that he could fill. For whatever reason, the two had responded to each other.

The teacher and I explained to Joey that he had to be quiet and gentle with the dog, or Devon would have to leave. Joey didn't pay much attention to me, but Charlene made contact by whispering into his ear. He did not want Devon to leave, so he did grow quieter. Devon, meanwhile, had barely moved a muscle. I saw no canine danger signals: no squirming or struggling, no panting or other signs of stress. Devon's ears weren't back; he wasn't growling or squinting or showing any teeth. In fact, he looked quite at home draped over this boy in a wheelchair.

So, keeping one eye on this odd duo, Charlene

maintaining vigilance, I switched on the mike and began to tell the waiting crowd about the fabled history of herding and the exploits of Carolyn MacWilki. And during much of the thirty-minute demonstration, Joey held my dog in his lap and the dog stayed contentedly with this child whose movements and mannerisms, as far as I knew, he'd never encountered before.

As for Homer, who hadn't cast a single glance at Joey, or at anyone else in the crowd, he was raring to go. Carolyn took over at the mike, while I opened the gate to the pen, sent Homer in to get the sheep, and had him pilot his small flock around the lawn and the hill for four or five minutes.

I looked over once and saw Devon step down from Joey's lap—Charlene helped Joey release him—and begin to visit the other kids from the school, accepting pats. But when Joey began to shout his name, Devon came quickly back to his side and stood there, putting his head in his lap, and Joey clapped and laughed. "De-thon! De-thon!" I could hear it up the hill where Homer and I were rounding up the sheep, who needed little persuasion to get back into the pen. When it was time to go, Joey cried and shouted all the way back to the van.

This was the most verbal and animated she'd seen Joey in some weeks, Charlene said. Was there any chance I could bring Devon to visit, while the encounter was still fresh in Joey's mind? Sure, I

247

said; we exchanged phone numbers and e-mail addresses.

Devon watched the van pull away, his eyes locked on the bus until it chugged out of sight. Homer had resettled himself by the pen, keeping fierce watch over his sheep. Two working dogs, I thought, one doing the very job he'd been bred for, another helping a severely retarded boy—for reasons I doubted I'd ever grasp—to open up, to speak, to connect with the world. The new work and the old.

I waited a few months before going back to learn what had happened to the Montclair people and dogs I'd spent time with. The return visits reaffirmed an early thought: the story of dogs and people is sometimes the story of life itself.

Rushmore, the German shepherd I'd met at Mills early on, didn't survive his owner's remarriage. As much as Kate DeLand believed the dog had enabled her to survive the death of her husband, she also perceived him as an obstacle to happiness with her new one. She didn't want to take that risk. She gave Rushmore to a German shepherd rescue group, which placed him in a home near New Paltz, New York. She assumed he was doing well; she hadn't checked.

Sandra Robinson was still struggling. Her nascent relationship with the programmer in Morristown hadn't worked out; he was too needy, she decided. She wanted to be a good mother, but not to him. Now her moods rose and fell as she realized the dimensions of the emotional issues she faced, the depression, the loneliness, the painful past. But she had made new friends and was getting out more. Ellie the dachshund had been an anchor, a fixed point. "She got me through," Sandra concluded.

Yet all was not well. Sandra told me that she and Ellie had reached a state she felt "a tad uncomfortable with. She has become very demanding and whiny. I am required to pay attention to her. It's either throwing the ball or wrestling, all the time." She could hardly manage to read, use the computer, or watch an episode of *The Sopranos*, she complained.

And that wasn't all: once mostly housebroken, Ellie had begun peeing in her apartment, on the carpet, even in her bed. Sandra concluded that the peeing was Ellie's revenge for not getting the attention she wanted.

Sandra was trying to recover from her crises, seeking out people, looking for work. She wanted the dog to grasp this sophisticated concept and behave accordingly.

Be careful, I wanted to warn Sandra: this was the moment when dogs get into trouble. Nobody can live happily with an unhousebroken dog, especially someone who believes the dog is acting out of spite. This is when dogs get given away, sent to shelters, whacked around.

After months of being cuddled and cooed over

virtually every minute, Ellie had become a bit of a bother. And just as suddenly, Ellie's love wasn't unconditional or uncritical. Sandra perceived her as angry, unappreciative.

Sandra had been treating Ellie more and more as a human—for several reasons, but particularly out of her wish to be a good mother. As a result, this dachshund had influence. If Sandra went out, it was because Ellie had somehow encouraged her to. If Sandra interrupted her work, it was because Ellie wanted to play and she couldn't refuse. If she met someone on the street, it was because Ellie had arranged it.

Increasingly, she seemed to attribute complex thoughts and ideas to the dog she'd come to see as the utterly devoted friend that analyst Dorothy Burlingham had written of.

In fact, whenever I talked to Sandra, Burlingham's description of the vulnerable, damaged child with the fantasy friend haunted me. This animal friend appears throughout literature and culture from *Little Lord Fauntleroy* to *Lassie* to *Old Yeller*. I saw in Sandra's relationship with her dog the yearning Burlingham described, "the child who owns an imaginary animal and never lacks companionship. . . . The two share everything, good and bad experiences, and complete understanding of each other; either speech is not necessary, or they have a secret language; the understanding between them goes beyond the realm of consciousness."

The dog's new behavioral problems and Sandra's

response left me feeling ambivalent, as was often the case. I wondered at the difficult work she perceived this little dog was doing on her behalf, but I felt saddened by her need for it. No dog could have lived up to her expectations for long.

In his book *In the Company of Animals*, James Serpell writes about our culture's tendency to denigrate some aspects of pet keeping. Loving a pet, as portrayed in mass media, is acceptable. Loving a dog or cat too much (and, Serpell points out, such excess is attributed more often to women than men) brands a person eccentric, antisocial, in some way deficient in human relationships. Yet there's no evidence that pet lovers have more problems with human relationships than anybody else, Serpell says.

If the intensity of Sandra's relationship with Ellie sometimes made me uneasy, I admired Sandra's bravery and determination, her willingness to approach, if slowly, the elemental truth about dogs: they aren't people. I believed she and Ellie had a shot at finding some peace and happiness.

The Divorced Dogs Club, as Rachel Goldner had predicted, broke apart as its members gradually recovered from their traumatic divorces and began the absorbing, painstaking work of rebuilding their lives. Some of the dogs in their group were rewarded for their devotion. Chester thrived with Janice's—and his—new soulmate. Her new partner tossed balls and Frisbees for the Lab, insisted he come along on weekend excursions, brought him bones from a local butcher and an $85 cedar bed from L.L. Bean with his name embroidered in gothic script. Sometimes, Janice exulted, the good guys won. Cynthia's Gusty was also thriving and had acquired a sister, another rescued greyhound.

Aviva, the pugnacious pug, moved with Rachel to a luxury condominium in neighboring West Orange. It broke Rachel's heart to leave the house she'd personally designed and still adored, but she gamely set about constructing her new life. Although she no longer had the wooded trails of Mills outside her back door, she and Aviva didn't really need them. The condo development encompassed seventy-five acres; the little pug had all the space she could want. Rachel seemed sadly, somewhat stubbornly resigned to the notion that she and Aviva would spend the rest of their days together in the duplex she was decorating with care and style. "I only hope she goes before me," Rachel said. "Otherwise it would be unbearable for her."

Carolyn had lost contact with the other Divorced Dogs Club members, but she wasn't hard to track down in Brooklyn, where she was still a freelance writer. Her Dalmatian, Sharpton, had troubles in his new Virginia home—too many aggressive encounters with her sister's other dogs. He'd moved on to a second home farther away. Carolyn hadn't heard anything from his new owners, so she gathered he was all right. "Truthfully," she admitted, "I'd rather not know if he wasn't. Too painful."

Did she feel that she owed him anything more? I wondered. She didn't. "I treated him well. I hope he's okay. But he *is* a dog."

Even as they scattered, the DDC members credited their dogs with providing emotional ballast in their lives at a time of critical need. To my mind, most of them would have regained their footing with or without a dog, but they didn't think so.

Betty Jean—still running her rescue group, still working past the point of fatigue, still undergoing tests for stomach pain, still rushing into Brooklyn a couple of times each week—was also still trying to raise $20,000 so she could quit her office job and rescue dogs full-time.

One change: her daughter realized it was time for a change in strategy. "It isn't that she doesn't love us. It's that she's so totally committed to this, for whatever reason," she told me. "If we want a relationship with her—and I do—we have to do it on her terms." So she brought her older kids over twice a week to help clean out the crates, play with the puppies, and take the smaller dogs into the yard.

"They love coming, and my mom seems to love having them," her daughter reported. "Frankly, I can't think of a better activity for kids. It's the one thing that pulls them off the computer."

The law firm where Rob Cochran worked was

suffering in a wobbly economy, so his days were a bit shorter and he walked Cherokee more than ever, taking longer treks to more remote spots, especially on weekends. He still refused to use treats regularly or train the dog more formally—he saw both as indulgent—but he was working harder to rein in the boisterous Lab. When he did use food, he actually got somewhere. When Cherokee lunged toward the curb, Rob sometimes tossed a few bits of kibble on the ground, and the dog was learning—"slowly"—to keep away from the street on their walks. Rob also occasionally peppered the ground with biscuits when passersby approached, so that Cherokee would head for the food, not their shoulders.

Rob couldn't stand to have a badly behaved dog, but given his own past, he really couldn't stand to discipline him, either. He saw that food worked, but thought using it wimpy, a kind of defeat. "The dog should do it for *me*," he said.

He was still thinking about how a dog could be, as he'd said, "more than a friend." The truth was, I already understood, all too well. In Rob and Cherokee I saw some of men's happiest and saddest traits simultaneously: their ingrained loneliness, even in the midst of family; their lack of meaningful friendships; their inability to talk openly, even with people who loved them; their loyalty, honesty, and steadfastness. I was glad Rob and Cherokee had each other, because, in some elemental ways, neither had anyone else.

Donna didn't get the time she hoped for to build her farmhouse in the country and live there with Harry, the big-eared corgi. But she already knew that life foils plans and fate takes its own course, despite the love of a good dog.

Her cancer spread, the pain and her weakness increased, and by midwinter she was largely bed-ridden, taking morphine intravenously when lesser painkillers could no longer do the job. She decided it would be best if Harry went to Joan's earlier than planned.

She felt she could no longer take proper care of him. She needed substantial doses of medication; her apartment drew a stream of health aides and hospice workers; she lacked the strength to walk Harry or play with him. "It's no life for a dog," she wisecracked, cheerful as always. "And I just can't stand the thought of saying goodbye to him. If I imagine it one more day, I think I'll just perish."

So Joan packed up Harry's things—his dog bed, favorite toys and bones, food and vitamins, along with his AKC papers and veterinary records and a picture Donna had taken of his now-legendary herding triumph. Donna wrote a check for $8,000 for what she called the Perpetual Harry Care Program. Joan didn't want any money, but Donna was adamant.

On the night he left, Donna and Joan told me afterward, Harry sensed something was up. He looked anxiously from Donna to Joan as she stacked his belongings by the door. Donna called him up on the bed, hugged him while he licked her face about fifty times, took a last picture, and then tearfully gestured to Joan to take him away. Joan put a leash on the big-eared corgi and urged him along.

Donna had written a farewell song for Harry, to the tune of "Happy Days Are Here Again," but she couldn't bring herself to sing it. She e-mailed me the the first verse, though:

Happy days will come again.
Harry and I will meet again.
We'll chase some sheep and eat some treats.
Happy days will come again . . .

Joan promised to sing it to him at the appropriate time.

Being tugged toward the door, Harry kept turning and looking back, his big brown eyes wide, his enormous ears almost flat against his head. But it really wasn't in his nature to be disobedient or put up much fight. So he followed Joan outside to her car.

Not wanting to upset him, Donna muffled her sobs with her pillow. Joan looked up from the street and saw the lights go out in the apartment.

A few weeks later, Joan reported that Harry was doing well. He hadn't eaten much for the first several days; he'd whimpered, moped, and paced in his new home. But after a few tough days, he slowly resumed eating and gnawing on rawhide toys. With a bit of coaxing, he slept on Joan's bed, watched TV on her lap, gobbled generous helpings of meatloaf, his favorite. He befriended the two mutts who lived next door and was regularly invited to play in their fenced yard. When she had to go to work, Joan popped a sheepherding videotape into her VCR; she reported that he sat transfixed in front of the TV.

Trainers and breeders know this particular trait of dogs, their adaptability. People find it unbearable to part with creatures they love so; they are sure the dogs feel the same way. But although we don't fully understand their minds, we do know that dogs have different notions of time and memory. Drawn into the sights, smells, and activities of their new environments, they adjust. They forget. As psychologist John Archer says, there's a reason that dogs have proven among the most adaptable and resourceful of all species.

Their ability to work in new ways, to love their humans dearly, is not in question. Harry's devotion to Donna was unwavering. But his transition demonstrated an important truth about dogs, though we are reluctant to accept it: they are different from us.

Joan and Donna had agreed not to talk about the dog unless something was wrong, but Joan broke her promise to report on how well he was doing. Sometimes, when she picked up his leash, Joan thought he seemed particularly excited. Maybe he thought he was going to see Donna. But for the most part, he was thriving.

Hard as it was to think of Harry living just a few miles away, Donna was nothing but happy and relieved to hear it. "I knew a woman once who arranged for her bulldog to be put down when she died," Donna told me. "What a selfish, self-centered person. I hated that idea. Harry is a great dog and he has many happy days left. Why wouldn't I want that for him? Look how many happy days he gave me."

Rudy the yellow Lab continued to spend much of his day in his backyard, secure behind a new wooden picket fence too high to jump. On weekends, to vary the routine, sometimes he spent a few hours tied to a giant maple tree on the front lawn. But the neighbors rarely saw him. Whereas they saw Chaos, Diane Winship's Belgian sheepdog, all the time, strolling contentedly through the neighborhood with his owner. Half the kids on the block and the regular UPS and Fed-Ex drivers all kept biscuits on hand for him.

Tom and Penny remained an odd but contented duo. Tom's deteriorating health mysteriously improved; I heard no further talk of surgery. In fact, in a salutary gesture toward the future, Tom took much of his savings and, without even alerting his landlord, paid for a chain-link fence to enclose the backyard so he could leave Penny outside on sunny days when he worked at the gas station. It cost him $1,300, the largest single expenditure he'd made in years, apart from his old LeSabre. "I felt like I owed it to her, she's been so good to me," he said. "Hell, some nursing home would get it otherwise."

When he left Penny in the yard, she positioned herself at the gate, from which she never moved and could see the street and bark at every skateboarder, bike rider, truck, school bus, pedestrian, or dog that passed.

Most pleasant evenings I saw them sitting on the stoop, Penny fending off real or imagined evildoers, protecting Tom. In cold or wet weather, the glow from the TV flickered through the front window and it was nice to know the two of them were together inside. Even over the TV, though, Penny barked at passersby. Sometimes I could hear Tom pleading, "Hey, come on, doll, be nice."

Jamal made the varsity basketball squad at Montclair High in the fall, a big achievement for him, and a big commitment. The team intended to get to the state finals; the coach expected discipline and work, good grades and faithful attendance at after-school and weekend practices.

Jamal and Alishia had a long talk and agreed that Dre ought to go to another home. But Jamal couldn't handle saying goodbye. It was a measure of Alishia's pride and support that she nervously dragged Dre from his room and, as agreed, drove him to PAWS, the local animal shelter.

He remained there for several weeks. The prospects of adoption, the shelter said, were not good.

Pit bulls didn't leave the shelter as often these days, as bad publicity about the breed and associated insurance problems mounted.

So I called Betty Jean, who made yet another policy exception and sent someone from Save the Pets to pick Dre up. She declared him "a cutie" and reported no ill effects from the daily beatings; he didn't need medical attention. She thought his new owner should be a single man or woman, preferably with no children. Pit bull rescuers were among the most devoted out there, she'd learned. She would find Dre a home. Meanwhile, he'd acquired a taste for salsa music.

As for Jamal, playing for the varsity team gave him some status, a new group of friends, and a developing relationship with his coach, who had teamed up with his English teacher to nag him about college. Alishia believed he was emerging from a difficult, potentially dangerous time, and she was grateful for the dog's role in that passage. But Jamal had never talked much about his problems, and if he missed Dre, he never said so. His mother said he never mentioned the dog again.

Mrs. Giamatti, still living alone in her Walnut Street apartment, expected her daughters to fly home over Christmas; the three of them would look at some assisted-care facilities, especially the one operated by the Catholic Church in Union County. She planned to move into whichever one they selected the following spring. "I want it to be my last move," she said. "I expect it will be." In general, her health was holding up, but walking had become progressively harder.

Trixie's ashes sat on her mantle in a small cardboard box. Mrs. Giamatti sadly missed her poodle. At least once a day, "I still reach down to pet her. But she's not there anymore."

The range of dogs' work these days is breathtaking: they join search-and-rescue missions, help the blind, guard property, sniff for bombs and illegal drugs, and comfort the elderly, the traumatized, the bereaved, and the lonely. Therapists enthusiastically enlist dogs in treating drug and alcohol addiction and in a broad range of rehabilitation work. They increasingly use dogs to help emotionally disturbed children.

If there is a cloud hanging over this work, it's that the fate of these animals is so varied, the results so difficult to measure, their work so often unrewarded.

In the two-feet-deep stack of books, studies, and journal articles I'd amassed relating to the bond between humans and dogs, hardly one addressed whether this new work was beneficial for our favored species. A couple suggested that giving dogs fewer opportunities to roam freely or problem-solve was making them dumber, but that was about it.

It's presumptuous to try to speak for another species, especially one that can't talk or even, in conventional terms, think. But I'd like to consider their new work from their perspective, as much as that's possible.

In *Pack of Two*, the late Carolyn Knapp's wonderful book about her relationship with a puppy named Lucille, she wrote that "dog owners like me are in closer emotional proximity to dogs these days because we understand them better . . . thanks in large part to the explosion of information about the nature of the dog, his heritage and his mind. My grandfather certainly didn't spend his leisure time cruising dog chat rooms on the Internet, or investigating canine Web pages, or attending online veterinary forums."

But my journey through Dogville, U.S.A., left me with other, sometimes sadder, notions about dogs' new roles. Dog owners like Knapp (and me) live in closer emotional proximity to dogs, I think, because we need them more than our grandfathers did. Because we are increasingly discontented, disaffected, isolated, needy. Because we are lonelier. Because we feel powerless and vulnerable, removed from the people who run our work and civic lives. Because many of us hate our work and resent the people who make it so insecure. Families scatter; friends can let us down. More and more, we've turned to dogs when we need love, or despair of unfulfilling lives, or face death.

Why not? Dogs are plentiful, dutiful, loving. Humans, we fear, won't or can't help us when we lose our jobs, find ourselves alone, grow sick or old. Dogs will at least try.

Nor can I share Knapp's sense that we are getting to know dogs better. Dogs have never been more regulated, controlled, and separated from humans than they are now—thus the longing apparent among the visitors to Carolyn Wilki's sheepherding demonstrations. Again and again, in my treks around Montclair, I was surprised by how *little* people knew or wanted to learn about their dogs.

If we really knew dogs, would we be attributing to them the vast, complex panoply of emotions that are unique to humans? See them as people when they are not? Would we overfeed and underwork them? Would we acquire large, active working dogs for small apartments or town houses in congested tracts? Would we refuse to train them? Beat and abandon them by the millions? Would we bar them from doing almost everything they naturally want and need to do, from roaming and sniffing to settling dog scores and chasing squirrels?

Perhaps it is and has always been the nature and fate of contemporary dogs to serve humans and then step aside or get left behind when their work is done. Many of us seem to feel that's the way we treat other humans now as well. Perhaps this fate is simply the price dogs pay for all the shelter, care, and affection they receive, a natural evolutionary extension of the time when dogs threw themselves in front of wild animals to protect their humans.

But I find it troubling, this idea that we can deny or alter the very nature of animals to suit our temporal needs, the arrogant assumption that an entire subordinate species exists solely to lend us a hand when we want help, often later to be discarded like junk-food wrappers when we don't. Yet it's clearly so, the reality of many dogs in our society.

I also had some nagging questions about how helpful, ultimately, dogs' new work was to some of the humans who demanded it. Could dogs truly provide all they were being asked to? Could they perform reliably as surrogate humans, even shrinks?

As Knapp acknowledges in her book, "man cannot live by dog alone." Her own dog, she wrote, "may have helped me get out of a relationship, but could she ever help me get *in* one? Or have I found in her some kind of alternative to adult intimacy, a less complex and demanding way of living with another being?" Where, she wonders, is the line between self-protection and self-limitation?

I had found myself wondering the same thing on my unexpectedly intense, sometimes jarring forays into the emotional landscape of people and their dogs.

I asked those questions when Sandra gave up on the idea of finding a suitable partner or being a loving mother and turned instead to a tiny puppy for companionship. And when Donna decided to end her life with a corgi. I certainly wondered about Jamal, who needed—and abused—a dog to help him feel safe and important. Yet I was also saddened to think of Mrs. Giamatti who, despite the love of two devoted daughters, sits, even now, alone by her window without Trixie.

Wandering around Dogville, I mulled how extraordinary it was that humans had no organizations run by people like Betty Jean. Why couldn't the lonely, the left-behind elderly, the divorced or bereft, the mentally impaired and the traumatized log onto websites like hers and be whisked off in vans by dedicated rescuers? Why couldn't people be taken in, nursed back to physical and emotional health, and given fuller, happier, more loving and meaningful lives in carefully chosen settings?

Shouldn't there be groups obsessed with helping abandoned *people*, helping to replace their mobile children or deceased spouses, repairing the damage left by their unhappy childhoods, making them whole and happy? Rescuers could screen their new lovers and partners, check on friends to ensure that they were loyal and wise, visit their charges' new homes to be sure they were properly cared for. They'd be available day and night, seven days a week; and if anything went wrong, if the new home didn't work out, the rescuers would repeat the entire process, building new lives for the lost and sad humans of our world.

Give dogs their bittersweet due: they're doing hard and sometimes thankless work. But that says something about us, our country, and our lives, something that doesn't often show up in media stories, glossy pet magazines, or picturesque slow-motion dog-food ads.

Explorations into this new work can be reaffirming, too. I remind myself that lots of people in Montclair and elsewhere live full and happy lives with dogs who simply hang around, play with the kids, keep a covetous eye on the garbage, and aren't involved in their humans' attachment issues or complex pasts. But if dogs' roles are a mirror of America, and I think they are, then they faithfully reflect its hard, disaffected, and increasingly lonely underside. Which doesn't make the new work of dogs less important—quite the opposite. Sometimes one wants to thank God they're around.

Perhaps we shower dogs with gourmet treats, toys, songs, birthday parties, and kisses out of guilt. We take from them the love we never got enough of; seek from them the security we can never truly have, and expect unconditional and uncritical devotion in return.

Apart from the dogs, there are reasons for people to be careful as well. Dr. Leonard J. Simon wrote about "The Pet Trap: Negative Effects of Pet Ownership on Families and Individuals" in the 1984 collection *The Pet Connection: Its Influence on Our Health and Quality of Life*. A psychoanalyst, Simon spoke with hundreds of people about their pets, and at times felt certain that the presence of a pet enabled them to survive a situation that might otherwise have destroyed them—as when a dog gave a child love his parents didn't.

But not everything he heard was benign. In some cases, Simon became convinced that certain individuals' lives would have unfolded differently, and probably for the better, if there had been no dog or cat. "All too often I heard of wasted years and stagnant lives in which almost everything a person did revolved around his animal. I heard of divorces that might never have happened and I heard of some that probably should have happened long before, and after the pet died they finally did. I heard of children that might have been born if there had been no pet. I heard of children that were bitten by dogs that had given clear signs of jealousy but whose owners were unable to part with them."

As a result of his investigations, Simon came to believe that the decision to bring a pet into one's life or family can be fraught with consequences. What makes the decision "different from many other life decisions is that for the most part we are unaware of (and usually unable to predict) the psychological changes it will produce in our lives."

Simon's caution rang especially true for me as I finished work on this book, looked back on all the people and dogs I'd seen. Getting a dog seems so innocuous compared to getting married or having a child. Perhaps that's why people seem to give it so little thought. The psychological impact is, nevertheless, unpredictable, and usually unexpected. Experiences do vary widely.

This, of course, takes us back into the realm of attachment theory, which explains so much about the new work of dogs and their interplay with people.

Attachment theory as it relates to dogs isn't theoretical, to my mind, but highly utilitarian; it can sometimes help us understand the relationship and connections between the two species. Understanding that our earliest emotional experiences were formative, that we connect with animals out of our own unanswered needs for security and affection, can help us to forge a more realistic and satisfying relationship with dogs.

It can help people decide whether to have a dog or not, guide them as to breed and disposition. It can provide breeders and shelter and rescue workers with tools to help decide which dogs really belong with which owners.

It can guide owners through the range of behavioral issues that all dogs bring with them, helping them to be clearer, more patient, and more effective in training. It can also help trainers understand some of the hidden issues they face as they struggle to help people with their dogs.

When the right dog connects with the right person for the right reason and there is clarity, self-awareness, and truth in the relationship, dogs are far more likely to be secure, happy, calm, and better behaved. Someone who understands attachment theory will see that crating a dog is not inherently cruel; that expensive toys and oven-baked biscuits that look like hot dogs fulfill human, not canine, needs; that leashing an aggressive dog is essential to the well-being and safety of the dog and others.

It could shed light on the epidemic phenomenon of dog abandonment. Something is seriously off kilter when 10 million dogs are in shelters and 5 million are euthanized each year.

The theory can even sometimes guide us through the grimmest decisions we make about our dogs: when to end their lives. Our inability to separate from our dogs, even if they're suffering or facing severely diminished quality of life or actually are comatose, also speaks to our own interests, not necessarily theirs.

Perhaps most significantly, understanding our own emotions can help us understand our dogs as they are, not as we need or want to see them. Understanding the issues that connect us to our dogs means that we can love them and be loved by them as much as we'd like—but we can also know more of the truth. We can see dogs as dogs and treat them as they need to be treated, rather than view them as—in the phrase one Montclair woman used—"children with fur."

The new work of dogs seems, in some measure, to have been triggered by the great need Americans have for more meaningful attachments than contemporary life often provides.

My wanderings through Dogville reminded me that, like fingerprints, each person, each dog, each relationship is unique. Countless factors play into the human-dog bond, from the person's income and education to the dog's breeding and previous experiences. No single theory can cover every dog and owner every time.

In his many studies on pet behavior and attachment, James Serpell of the Veterinary School of the University of Pennsylvania has explored the expectations humans have of their "ideal" dog. Most people, Serpell observes, want their dogs to be very playful, confident, and relaxed in unfamiliar situations, intensely affectionate, well-behaved, and obedient yet also active and energetic, friendly, and approachable with strangers, not to mention intelligent, quiet, and clean. They also want their dogs to accept being alone, and to avoid aggressive behavior.

Such "ideal" dogs—dogs who act like well-behaved humans—are perceived more positively by their owners. "Actual" dogs—who behave more like dogs—generate much lower levels of affection from their owners.

Serpell's research says a lot about the dogs' complex and sometimes fragile situation in a changing America. As long as they meet our rising expectations of their nature and behavior—that is to say, as long as they love us uncritically and don't frighten us or our friends—we will love them in return. When they don't behave that way, it's a different story. It's almost like telling your child: "I will love and take care of you as long as you are clean, friendly, well-adjusted, get straight A's, score soccer goals, and everybody likes you. But if you have any problems, we'll send you away to another family."

Serpell cites a 1984 study of people relinquishing dogs to animal shelters in the United States. "Behavior problems" was the second most common reason people gave for disowning their pets.

That's quite ironic, considering how few dogs receive professional training—according to one veterinary association study, fewer than 5 percent. People want their dogs to arrive in "ideal" form. But they are reluctant to spend time and money (they can also, of course, learn to train their dogs inexpensively themselves) to show them how to behave.

Self-awareness—and emotional responsibility—can help remind us that dogs are not human, a crucial distinction for their welfare and ours. Well-meaning but dangerous thoughtlessness causes trouble for dogs and the people who own and live near them.

Even in the sensitive environs of Montclair, I saw a growing and disturbing array of weapons sold and deployed to force dogs to be more "ideal," from choke chains and restraining muzzles to pronged collars, shock collars, electronic fences, and devices that spray stinging chemicals into dogs' eyes when they bark. The pet industry has obviously figured out that most people don't want to, or know how to, train their dogs, but they'll invest in shortcuts.

More common was the sight of people scolding and shouting at their dogs, repeating disobeyed commands and constantly tugging and jerking at their dogs' leashes. The tension between people and their dogs—even people who love their dogs a lot—was often disheartening. But it underscored the truth: that they are not like us. They are not like children. They possess alien minds. They are not truly members of our family. They are animals that sometimes mean the world to us. But they are moons, not suns: they revolve around us and our lives; they're not meant to occupy the center.

Dogs are wondrous in their own right, but in different ways than people are. When we forget that, and forget the complex emotions and experiences we bring to our relationships with dogs, we—and, especially, they—get into trouble.

Yet it's unlikely that Americans will undertake a rational civic debate regarding dog issues. The national political agenda has more pressing concerns these days, and the thousands of ferocious local battles about dogs are largely uninformed. All we can realistically do, therefore, is take it one dog at a time. We can learn as much as we can about our dogs and ourselves, our motives and their needs, and do the best we can with our own animals.

What I saw in Dogville was that we are with our dogs as we were shaped ourselves. We bring to them the emotions we encountered—our deepest yearnings, fears, needs, frustrations, angers, and, most universally, our instinctive desire to attach to entities that we love and will love us. Our mounting needs and anxieties bring out the best and worst in the dog-owning experience, and reveal the best and worst in us.

Three days after the Scottish and Irish Festival, Devon, Homer, and I pulled up, as promised, to a small two-story wood-frame house outside Easton, Pennsylvania. This was a "pod" house, one of several residences for students at a local school for the severely disabled.

Between six and a dozen kids lived here, along with a driver, a health aide, and, part of the time, a trained social worker. The teachers, who lived elsewhere, came and went. The idea was that residents wouldn't feel institutionalized, but could live, shop, and sometimes work in a wider community.

The house was tidy, but the street was depressing, a landscape of empty lots, a few tattered stores, a factory of some sort.

This was where Joey lived, where his parents had reluctantly sent him when he became too strong and agitated for them to manage at home, the place he'd returned to after meeting Devon at the herding demonstration.

I brought Homer along, too; frankly, I'd always thought of him as the more social of the two dogs, the most reliable around kids and strangers, unfailingly sweet to all creatures but sheep.

Charlene was waiting for us with a sheaf of artwork and markings, Joey's writings and drawings about Devon. His encounter with the dog had triggered an unprecedented outpouring of speaking, writing, and drawing, she said excitedly, more than she'd seen from Joey before. She'd called his parents to tell them about his response, and they were excited, too. They hoped Devon might become a regular part of Joey's routine. Although still wary about this prospect, so did I. What could be more satisfying for the owner of any dog, working breed or not, than to help a kid like Joey open up and communicate?

Joey was waiting for us in the yard, so we followed Charlene through the house, past two or three of the other residents, who began shouting, clapping, and moving toward the dogs. Homer's ears went back; he looked spooked.

It might eventually be possible to desensitize him to such noises and movements, but not then and there. So we turned back to my truck and I put Homer in the rear seat. Then Devon and I went back inside. He, too, seemed unnerved by the uproar, but not so much as Homer had been.

Out back, Joey, who'd been told we were coming, was wearing the same clothes (minus the baseball cap) and holding a child's plastic spill-proof milk cup. He yelled when he saw Devon, and threw the cup at him, a reflex.

Devon jumped when the cup thumped his shoulder, and backed quickly to the door, looking at me. I threw him a few bits of beef jerky; food often calmed Devon. He relaxed, and then, watching Joey, maybe remembering him, his tail started to swish. Charlene stood by Joey's wheelchair and reminded him to be gentle or the dog would have to go away.

"De-thon! De-thon!" Joey shouted. Devon walked up to the wheelchair, tail wagging, and licked Joey's hand. This time he didn't jump into the boy's lap, but plopped down on the grass next to his wheelchair, where Joey could reach over and stroke him. Charlene once again guided his hand, showing him how to pet Devon calmly. I tossed Devon some food, then sat down in a lawn chair across the yard.

It was startling to see this excitable creature, a dog who normally wouldn't leave my side, sitting as if fastened to the wheelchair of a disabled boy who suddenly loved him. The two seemed to connect in ways I couldn't explain. Over a couple of minutes, Joey quieted, a bright and happy smile radiating from his face. Devon lay almost immobile, as comfortable and as calm as I'd ever seen him. I felt sure he knew he was working. He seemed to be bringing as much focus and determination to this visit as Homer did to herding sheep.

Later, Charlene, also amazed at the rapport between them, asked me what I thought the dog was up to. "Do you think he senses the need in Joey?"

I wish I could have said yes and believed it; I was tempted to. But I also knew that Devon had some spectacular issues of his own. Raised by a previous owner to compete in obedience trials, he'd been rigorously trained, had failed and been supplanted, then abandoned and sent away. When I took him in, he attached himself to me like a leech; in our first weeks, he'd jump out a window to follow me if I left him.

Much of the work of the past two years had focused on teaching him how to feel secure, when I was there and when I wasn't. He still watched me like a hawk, craved attention, nuzzled poor Homer aside when anybody's hand reached out for a pat, pushed into the bed between my wife and me. Devon would even, given a choice, forgo sheep to stand beside me, something few border collies in the world would do.

And Joey was shouting Devon's name, focusing on the dog with remarkable intensity. I suspected Devon, who might never outgrow his need for attention, was responding to that.

No, Charlene insisted, you're underestimating the dog. He's working at it. He's connecting to Joey. It's wonderful to see. In her assessment, I sensed the Disney dog, the heroic canine rushing to the aid of a troubled kid.

Maybe she was right, I thought as we drove away. Maybe I was clinging to cynical notions about dog behavior. Did it really matter what Devon's motivitations were? What counted here was the obvious good he was doing Joey, the good we expected him to keep doing for this needy child in the coming months.

What was fascinating was that Devon—my dog, my own source of unconditional love, my Dorothy Burlingham-style special friend—seemed to be switching careers before my eyes. Turning away from the ancient art of herding sheep, never as much his forte as it was Homer's, he had jumped with four feet into the new work of dogs. Yet I knew that his most important work, more than herding or visiting Joey, was helping me.

Raspberry Ridge, Carolyn Wilki's sheep farm and dog training center, was less than a half hour from Joey's house. I put Devon in his crate and went out with Homer to take the notoriously difficult and rebellious ram lambs to pasture. These male lambs were nothing like the older, more docile South Downs, which were "dog-broke." There were about a dozen, born the previous spring, and they didn't flock together when dogs approached, but ran, hid, butted the dogs, dove into the thorny underbrush.

I'd seen more than one dog, including both of mine, collapse in near exhaustion after chasing ram lambs. But Carolyn thought Homer should give it a shot.

Released from their pens, the troublesome lambs

scattered immediately, wanting no part of being herded. They dashed behind the barn, then broke for the woods and thickets—too thorny for me to go in after them. But Homer pursued them gamely. For more than an hour in the strong sun, he waded in and drove out one lamb after another, emerging with burrs and twigs clinging to his fur. He was limping on sore pads, he was panting, and several times I reached for the walkie-talkie to radio Carolyn for help.

But Homer showed no signs of quitting, and I didn't want to quit on him. Each time I grabbed the radio, a lamb popped out of the undergrowth, Homer plowing steadily behind it.

It was an almost spiritual experience to watch these faithful old instincts rise up in my young dog as he corralled the renegade lambs, headed them off, anticipated their flight. To my great surprise, as I walked down the trail to the pasture, Homer was sitting proudly by the flock, holding them in place as they grazed. They seemed to have given up the battle and accepted his authority. Or maybe they were just hungry.

I couldn't help thinking what this kind of dedication might have meant to a farmer in Ireland generations earlier. Homer's tongue was hanging nearly to the ground, and his paws were bloodied, but with little direction from me, he'd figured out what he had to do and refused to give up until he'd done it.

Afterward, the sheep back in their pen—another

fight—I let Devon out. He glanced toward the sheep, then went down on his front paws, challenging Homer to play, an invitation Homer, however exhausted, never passed up.

The two dogs raced around the farm in widening circles, chasing after squirrels and rabbits and each other, their enthusiasm and energy so infectious and joyous I laughed out loud. It was deeply satisfying to see these beautiful creatures play as hard as they worked.

They'd surprised me, and not for the last time. Carolyn cautioned me not to pigeonhole my dogs and their work. Over the next few weeks and months, Homer ended up in Joey's lap more than once, and Devon got more interested in sheep. Dogs and their tasks are works in progress.

ACKNOWLEDGMENTS

For *The New Work of Dogs* I am in the debt of more people than I've ever had to acknowledge in my previous eleven books, which were more solitary affairs.

First off, my wife, Paula Span, has sacrificed countless hours, listened to more chatter about dogs than she ever wanted to hear, and helped significantly with the conception, writing, and editing of this book. My daughter, Emma Span, has evolved from a great kid into a trusted and admired friend.

Richard Abate of ICM provided creativity, leadership, support, and guidance.

Bruce Tracy's patience, support, high tolerance for craziness, and deft editing have helped me enormously.

Brian McLendon long ago became more than a publicist; he's a valued counselor.

Carolyn Wilki of the Raspberry Ridge Sheep Farm and Training Center in Bangor, Pennsylvania, is not only a friend but a teacher and an inspiration.

For all its ups and downs, the Internet is a miracle sometimes, never more so than when it connects people like me with people like Dr. Debra Katz, Director of Residency Training, Department of Psychiatry, at the University of Kentucky in Lexington. She's been a huge influence on this book and on my thinking about dogs, humans, and their relationship to one another. She's become a friend as well.

I am grateful to Lesli Broyles, Kathie King, and, especially, to Tag Heister of the University of Kentucky for the invaluable research they have unearthed for me.

I am in the debt of many people who have shared their experiences with dogs and taught me so much about them, especially Karen Simpson and Reggie, John and Cynthia Palmer and Boomer, and Ove Nymberg and Spirit. And Dave, a great man. I again thank Margaret Waterson of the Battenkill Book Shop in Cambridge, New York, for first suggesting that I write about dogs. She has set me on a happy course.

I am grateful to the people who brought me into the dog rescue world—many of whom insist on remaining nameless—for spending so much time with me, and for permitting me to observe and experience this extraordinary subculture.

I thank Montclair Township Manager Terence Reidy for his help and information regarding the township's dogs. And Dr. Brenda King for letting me hang out in her veterinary practice and for sharing some of her experiences and insights. Thanks also to Dr. Matt Mason, Mary Todd, and Dr. Paul Hartunian, especially helpful at the beginning of my research into this book.

I thank Joel Tabor of Montclair Pet and Feed Supply for his love of dogs and for connecting me to dog owners and providing his own invaluable expertise. And Kate Hamilton.

I thank the many people I interviewed and spent time with, whose homes and lives I entered.

I am indebted, too, to many authors, researchers, and publications. Some I drew on (and credited) extensively; others simply challenged or informed me. While I don't share all their opinions, I found their work useful and include them here for those who might be interested in pursuing their ideas further.

Among the books I've relied on:

Robert D. Putnam, *Bowling Alone: The Collapse and Revival of American Community* (Simon & Schuster, 2000); Susan J. Pharr and Robert Putnam, eds., *Disaffected Democracies: What's Troubling the Trilateral Countries?* (Princeton University Press, 2000); Richard Sennett, *The Corrosion of Character: The Personal Consequences of Work in the New Capitalism* (Norton, 1998); John Bowlby, *Attachment* (Basic Books, 1969); Dr. Peter Fonagy, *Attachment Theory and Psychoanalysis* (Other Press, 2001); Stanley Coren, *The Pawprints of History: Dogs and the Course of Human Events* (Free Press, 2002); Patricia B. McConnell, Ph.D., *The Other End of the Leash: Why We Do What We Do Around Dogs* (Ballantine Books, 2002); Caroline Knapp, *Pack of Two: The Intricate Bond Between*

People and Dogs (Delta, 1999); Elizabeth Marshall Thomas, *The Hidden Life of Dogs* (Pocket Books, 1993); Stephen Budiansky, *The Truth about Dogs: An Inquiry into the Ancestry, Social Conventions, Mental Habits, and Moral Fiber of* Canis familiaris (Viking, 2000); Pat Miller, *The Power of Positive Dog Training* (Howell House Books, 2001); Dr. Marty Becker, *The Healing Power of Pets: Harnessing the Amazing Ability of Pets to Make and Keep People Healthy and Happy* (Hyperion, 2002); Marjorie Garber, *Dog Love* (Simon & Schuster, 1997).

I also found these academic and research works to be invaluable:

Dorothy Burlingham, *Twins* (International University Press, 1952); Alexa Albert and Kris Bulcroft, "Pets, Families, and the Life Course," *Journal of Marriage and the Family*, May 1988; Karl Heinz Brisch, Kenneth Kronenberg, and Lotte Kohler, *Treating Attachment Disorders* (Guilford Press, 2002); National Council on Pet Population Study and Policy (www.petpopulation.org/statsurvey.html); Rebecca Gardyn, "Animal Magnetism," *American Demographics*, May 2002; Pat Sable, "Pets, Attachment, and Well-Being Across the Life Cycle," *Social Work*, May 1995; E. K. Rynearson, "Humans and Pets and Attachment," *British Journal of Psychiatry*, vol. 133, 1978; John Archer, "Why Do People Love Their Pets?" *Evolution and Human Behavior*, vol. 18, 1997; Humane Society of the United States (www.hsus.org), "The Crisis of Pet

Overpopulation"; Marcel Heiman, M.D., "The Relationship Between Man and Dog," presented before the New York Psychoanalytic Society, June 10, 1952; J. C. Berryman, K. Howells, and M. Lloyd-Evans, "Pet Owner Attitudes to Pets and People: A Psychological Study," *Veterinary Record*, December 21–28, 1985; American Veterinary Medical Association, Center for Information Management, "Dog Ownership in the United States, 1996" (www.avma.org); Ivan Sherrick, "The Significance of Pets for Children," *Psychoanalytic Study of the Child*, 36, 1981; Edna Adelson and Vivian Shapiro, "Ghosts in the Nursery: A Psychoanalystic Approach to the Problems of Impaired Infant-Mother Relationships," from a lecture given at the Beata Rank Memorial Lecture Series, Boston Psychoanalytic Society and Institute, May 1974; Kenneth M. G. Keddie, "Pathological Mourning after the Death of a Domestic Pet," *British Journal of Psychiatry*, vol. 131, 1977.

Also Lenore C. Terr, "Childhood Traumas: An Outline and Overview," *American Journal of Psychiatry*, January 1991; Aaron H. Esman, "Rescue Fantasies," *Psychoanalytic Quarterly*, 56, 1987; Victoria L. Voith, John C. Wright, and Peggy J. Danneman, "Is There a Relationship Between Canine Behavior Problems and Spoiling Activities, Anthropomorphism, and Obedience Training?" *Applied Animal Behavior Science*, 34, 1992; Victoria Voith, "Attachment of People to Companion Animals," *Veterinary Clinics of North America: Small*

Animal Practice, March 1985; J. Topal, A. Miklosi, and V. Csanyi, "How Dog-Human Relationship Affects Problem Solving in the Dog," *Anthrozoos*, 10(4), 1997; James Serpell, "Evidence for an Association Between Pet Behavior and Owner Attachment Levels," *Applied Animal Behavior Science*, 47, 1996; Janet Haggerty Davis and Anne McCreary Juhasz, "The Preadolescent/Pet Bond and Psychological Development," in Marvin B. Sussman, ed., *Pets and the Family* (Haworth Press, 1985); Peter R. Messent and James A. Serpell, "An Historical and Biological View of the Pet-Owner Bond," in Bruce Fogle, ed., *Interrelations Between People and Pets* (Charles C. Thomas, 1981); Leonard J. Simon, "The Pet Trap: Negative Effects of Pet Ownership on Families and Individuals," in Robert K. Anderson, Benjamin L. Hart, and Lynette A. Hart, *The Pet Connection: Its Influence on Our Health and Quality of Life*, Minneapolis Center to Study Human-Animal Relationships and Environments, 1984.

ABOUT THE AUTHOR

Jon Katz has written twelve books—six novels and six works of nonfiction. A two-time finalist for the National Magazine Award, he has written for *The New York Times*, *The Wall Street Journal*, *Rolling Stone*, and *Wired*. He is a contributing editor to public radio's *Marketplace* and to *Bark* magazine. A member of the Association of Pet Dog Trainers, he lives in northern New Jersey with his wife, Paula Span, a reporter for *The Washington Post*, their college-student daughter, Emma Span, and their two dogs. Katz is working on his next book, which is about women and dogs. He can be e-mailed at jonkatz3@comcast.net.